PLOTINUS
ENNEAD I.5

On Whether Well-Being Increases with Time

Translation with an Introduction and Commentary

DANIELLE A. LAYNE

PARMENIDES PUBLISHING
Las Vegas | Zurich | Athens

For Bracko and Shay Shay
If ever a two lived in the present moment
it was you

PARMENIDES PUBLISHING
Las Vegas | Zurich | Athens

This edition published in 2023 by Parmenides Publishing
in the United States of America

ISBN soft cover: 978-1-7335357-4-8
ISBN e-Book: 978-1-7335357-5-5

Library of Congress Cataloging-in-Publication Data

Names: Plotinus, author. | Layne, Danielle A., translator.
Title: Ennead I.5 : on whether well-being increases with time / Plotinus ; translation with an Introduction and commentary, Danielle A. Layne.
Other titles: Ennead. I, 5. English
Description: Las Vegas : Parmenides Publishing, [2023] | Series: The Enneads of Plotinus with philosophical commentaries | Includes bibliographical references and indexes. | Summary: "In Ennead I.5 Plotinus attempts to navigate a well-trodden path of inquiry by responding directly to a wide spectrum of popular theories on human flourishing, insisting emphatically that well-being belongs to the present moment. One of his central targets is Aristotle, who insisted that well-being be measured by "a complete life" or a life measured by virtue, a modus vivendi sustained via the development of appropriate habits (hexis) and the avoidance of misfortunes. At the same time the Hellenistic schools-with their insistence that happiness is available to practitioners in the immediacy of the "now"-take pride of place in Plotinus' short screed on the subject. This treatment provides an in-depth analysis of Plotinus' unique conception of the value of the present moment by highlighting Plotinus' dialogue with Aristotle and Hellenistic conceptions of the soul, pleasure and pain, and time and eternity"-- Provided by publisher.
Identifiers: LCCN 2023021248 (print) | LCCN 2023021249 (ebook) | ISBN 9781733535748 (paperback) | ISBN 9781733535755 (ebook)
Subjects: LCSH: Plotinus--Translations into English. | Happiness. | Aristotle--Influence. | Philosophy, Ancient.
Classification: LCC B693.E52 E5 2023 (print) | LCC B693.E52 (ebook) | DDC
185--dc23/eng/20230720
LC record available at https://lccn.loc.gov/2023021248
LC ebook record available at https://lccn.loc.gov/2023021249

Typeset in Warnock and Futura by Parmenides Publishing
Printed digitally by Integrated Books International (IBI), Chicago, IL

www.parmenides.com

Contents

Introduction to the Series With a Brief Outline of the Life and Thought of Plotinus (205–270 CE)

Plotinus was born in 205 CE in Egypt of Greek-speaking parents. He attended the philosophical schools in Alexandria where he would have studied Plato (427–347 BCE), Aristotle (384–322 BCE), the Stoics and Epicureans as well as other Greek philosophical traditions. He began his serious philosophical education, however, relatively late in life, at the age of twenty-seven and was deeply impressed by the Platonist Ammonius Saccas about whom we, unfortunately, know very little, but with whom Plotinus studied for some eleven years. Even our knowledge of Plotinus' life is limited to what we can glean from Porphyry's introduction to his edition of his philosophical treatises, an account colored by Porphyry's own concerns. After completing his studies in Alexandria Plotinus attempted, by joining a military expedition of the Roman emperor Gordian III, to make contact with the

Brahmins in order to learn something of Indian thought. Unfortunately Gordian was defeated and killed (244). Plotinus somehow managed to extract himself and we next hear of him in Rome where he was able to set up a school of philosophy in the house of a high-ranking Roman lady by the name of Gemina. It is, perhaps, surprising that he had no formal contacts with the Platonic Academy in Athens, which was headed at the time by Longinus, but Longinus was familiar with his work, partly at least through Porphyry who had studied in Athens. The fact that it was Rome where Plotinus set up his school may be due to the originality of his philosophical activity and to his patrons. He clearly had some influential contacts, not least with the philhellenic emperor Gallienus (253–268), who may also have encouraged his later failed attempt to set up a civic community based on Platonic principles in a ruined city in Campania.

Plotinus' school was, like most ancient schools of philosophy, relatively small in scale, but did attract distinguished students from abroad and from the Roman upper classes. It included not only philosophers but also politicians and members of the medical profession who wished to lead the philosophical life. His most famous student was Porphyry (233–305) who, as a relative latecomer to the school, persuaded him to put into writing the results of his seminars. It is almost certain that we possess most, if not all, of his written output, which represents his mature thought, since he didn't commence writing until the age of forty-eight. The school seemingly had inner and outer circles, and Plotinus himself was clearly an inspiring and sympathetic teacher who took a deep interest in the philosophical and spiritual progress of his students. Porphyry tells us that when he was suffering from severe depression Plotinus straight away visited him in his lodgings to help him. His concern for others is also illustrated by the fact that he was entrusted with the personal education of many orphans and the care of their property and careers. The reconciliation of this worldly involvement with the encouragement to lead a life of contemplation is encapsulated in Porphyry's comment that "he was present to himself and others at the same time."

The *Enneads* of Plotinus is the edition of his treatises arranged by his pupil Porphyry who tried to put shape to the collection he had inherited by organizing it into six sets of nine treatises (hence the name *"Enneads")* that led the reader through the levels of Plotinus' universe, from the physical world to Soul, Intellect and, finally, to the highest principle, the One. Although Plotinus undoubtedly had a clearly structured metaphysical system by the time he began committing himself to expressing his thought in written form, the treatises themselves are not systematic expositions, but rather explorations of particular themes and issues raised in interpreting Plato and other philosophical texts read in the School. In fact, to achieve his neat arrangement Porphyry was sometimes driven even to dividing certain treatises (e.g., III.2–3; IV.3–5, and VI.4–5).

Although Plotinus' writings are not transcripts of his seminars, but are directed to the reader, they do, nevertheless, convey the sort of lively debate that he encouraged in his school. Frequently he takes for granted that a particular set of ideas is already familiar as having been treated in an earlier seminar that may or may not be found in the written text. For this reason it is useful for the reader to have some idea of the main philosophical principles of his system as they can be extracted from the *Enneads* as a whole.

Plotinus regarded himself as a faithful interpreter of Plato whose thought lies at the core of his entire project. But Plato's thought, whilst definitive, does according to Plotinus require careful exposition and clarification, often in the light of other thinkers such as Aristotle and the Stoics. It is because of this creative application of different traditions of ancient thought to the interpretation of Plato that Plotinus' version of Platonism became, partly through the medium of later Platonists such as Porphyry, Iamblichus (245–325), and Proclus (412–485), an influential source and way of reading both Plato and Aristotle in the Middle Ages, the Renaissance, and up to the early 19th century, when scholars first began to differentiate Plato and "Neoplatonism." His thought, too, provided early Christian theologians of the Latin and particularly of the Byzantine tradition, with a rich variety of metaphysical concepts with which to explore and express difficult doctrinal ideas. His fashioning of Plato's ideas into a consistent metaphysical structure, though no longer accepted as a uniquely valid way of approaching Plato, was influential in promoting the notion of metaphysical systems in early modern philosophy. More recently increasing interest has centered on his exploration of the self, levels of consciousness, and his expansion of discourse beyond the levels of normal ontology to the examination of what lies both above and beneath being. His thought continues to challenge us when confronted with the issue of humanity's nature and role in the universe and of the extent and limitations of human knowledge.

Whilst much of Plotinus' metaphysical structure is recognizably an interpretation of Plato it is an interpretation that is not always immediately obvious just because it is filtered through several centuries of developing Platonic thought, itself already overlaid with important concepts drawn from other schools. It is, nevertheless, useful as a starting point to see how Plotinus attempts to bring coherence to what he believed to be a comprehensive worldview expressed in the Platonic dialogues. The Platonic Forms are central. They become for him an intelligible universe that is the source and model of the physical universe. But aware of Aristotle's criticism of the Platonic Forms as lifeless causes he takes on board Aristotle's concept of god as a self-thinker to enable him to identify this intelligible universe as a divine Intellect that thinks itself as the Forms or Intelligibles. The doctrine of the Forms as the thoughts of god had already entered Platonism, but not as the rigorously argued identity that Plotinus proposed. Moreover the Intelligibles, since they are identical with Intellect, are themselves actively intellectual; they are intellects. Thus Plato's world of Forms has become a complex and dynamic intelligible universe in which unity and plurality, stability, and activity are reconciled.

Now although the divine Intellect is one it also embraces plurality, both because its thoughts, the Intelligibles, are many and because it may itself be analyzed into thinker and thought. Its unity demands a further principle, which is the cause of its unity. This principle, which is the cause of all unity and being but does not possess unity or being in itself, he calls the One, an interpretation of the Idea of the Good in Plato's *Republic* that is "beyond being" and that may be seen as the simple (hence "one") source of all reality. We thus have the first two of what subsequently became known as the three Hypostases, the One, Intellect, and Soul, the last of which acts as an intermediary between the intelligible and physical universes. This last Hypostasis takes on all the functions of transmitting form and life that may be found in Plato, although Plato himself does not always make such a clear distinction between soul and intellect. Thus the One is the ultimate source of all, including this universe, which is then prefigured in Intellect and transmitted through Soul to become manifest as our physical universe. Matter, which receives imperfectly this expression, is conceived not as an independently existing counter-principle, a dangerously dualist notion, but is in a sense itself a product of the One, a kind of non-being that, while being nothing specific in itself, nevertheless is not simply not there.

But this procession from an ultimate principle is balanced by a return movement at each level of reality that fully constitutes itself only when it turns back in contemplation of its producer. And so the whole of reality is a dynamic movement of procession and return, except for matter, which has no life of its own to make this return; it is inert. This movement of return, which may be traced back to the force of "love" in Plato or Aristotle's final cause, is characterized by Plotinus as a cognitive activity, a form of contemplation, weaker at each successive level, from Intellect through discursive reasoning to the merest image of rational order as expressed in the objects of the physical universe.

The human individual mirrors this structure to which we are all related at each level. For each of us has a body and soul, an intellect, and even something within us that relates to the One. While it is the nature of soul to give life to body, the higher aspect of our soul also has aspirations toward intellect, the true self, and even beyond. This urge to return corresponds to the cosmic movement of return. But the tension between soul's natural duty to body and its origins in the intelligible can be, for the individual, a source of fracture and alienation in which the soul becomes over-involved and overwhelmed by the body and so estranged from its true self. Plotinus encourages us to make the return or ascent, but at the same time attempts to resolve the conflict of duties by reconciling the two-fold nature of soul as life-giving and contemplative.

This is the general framework within which important traditional philosophical issues are encountered, discussed and resolved, but always in a spirit of inquiry and ongoing debate. Issues are frequently encountered in several different contexts, each angle providing a different insight. The nature of the soul and its relationship to the body is examined at length (IV) using the Aristotelian distinctions of levels of soul (vegetative, growth, sensitive, rational) whilst maintaining the immortal nature of the transcendent soul in Platonic terms. The active nature of the soul in sense-perception is maintained to preserve the principle that incorporeals cannot be affected by corporeal reality. A vigorous discussion (VI.4 and 5) on the general nature of the relationship of incorporeals to body explores in every detail and in great depth the way in which incorporeals act on body. A universe that is the product of design is reconciled with the freedom of the individual. And, not least, the time-bound nature of the physical universe and human reason is grounded in the life of Intellect, which subsists in eternity. Sometimes, however, Plotinus seems to break outside the framework of traditional metaphysics: the nature of matter and the One, each as non-being, though in a different sense, strains the terminology and structure of traditional ontology; and the attempt to reconcile the role of the individual soul within the traditional Platonic distinction of transcendent and immanent reality leads to a novel exploration of the nature of the self, the "I."

It is this restless urge for exploration and inquiry that lends to the treatises of Plotinus their philosophical vitality. Whilst presenting us with a rich and complexly coherent system, he constantly engages us in philosophical inquiry. In this way each treatise presents us with new ideas and fresh challenges. And, for Plotinus, every philosophical engagement is not just a mental exercise but also contributes to the rediscovery of the self and our reintegration with the source of all being, the Platonic aim of "becoming like god."

While Plotinus, like Plato, always wishes to engage his audience to reflect for themselves, his treatises are not easy reading, partly no doubt because his own audience was already familiar with many of his basic ideas and, more importantly, had been exposed in his seminars to critical readings of philosophical texts that have not survived to our day. Another problem is that the treatises do not lay out his thought in a systematic way but take up specific issues, although always the whole system may be discerned in the background. Sometimes, too, the exact flow of thought is difficult to follow because of an often condensed mode of expression.

Because we are convinced that Plotinus has something to say to us today, we have launched this series of translations and commentaries as a means of opening up the text to readers with an interest in grappling with the philosophical issues revealed by an encounter with Plotinus' own words and arguments. Each volume will contain a new translation, careful summaries of the arguments and structure of the treatise, and a philosophical commentary that will aim to throw light on the philosophical meaning and import of the text.

John M. Dillon
Andrew Smith

Acknowledgments

I AM PRIMARILY INDEBTED to Gonzaga University and my colleagues for their help and support as I plugged away at this small but difficult project. I am ever grateful to Sara Wear, Edward Butler, Tyler Tritten, and François Renaud for reading and commenting on drafts of the commentary and translation. Andrew Smith and John Dillon were the finest of editors, smoothing out confusions and finding my notorious typos. I accept full responsibility for any errors that may remain, as I cannot expect them to have been superheroes, supererogatory as they might be. Finally, I would be remiss if I did not thank my family, particularly my lovely boys, Simon and Dante Felix, for whom I wish true joy and a spirit of constant wonderment. This project was finished just before the coronavirus pandemic. In point of fact, the last major edits for this essay were made in Italy February 2020 while I was teaching for the Gonzaga-in-Florence program. As news rolled in about the impending crisis, I watched as one of the most beautiful cities in the world shut down, streets suddenly filled with quiet fear and uncertainty—a microcosmic image of what would unexpectantly become the new normal for the entire world. It broke my heart to see how quickly we all slipped into a collective state of anxiety, wondering, waiting, and hoping to return to the joys of life pre-pandemic. In the end, I hope Plotinus' words on human happiness remind us of the abundance we have yet available to us right now and for always.

Introduction to the Treatise

In *On Whether Well-Being Increases with Time* Plotinus attempts to navigate a well-trodden path of inquiry by directly responding to a wide spectrum of popular theories on human flourishing, insisting emphatically that well-being belongs to the present moment. Indeed, Aristotle, with his insistence that well-being be measured by "a complete life" (*Nicomachean Ethics* 1098a16–20) or a life measured by virtue, a *modus vivendi* sustained via the development of appropriate habits (*hexis*) and the avoidance of misfortunes, is one of Plotinus' central targets. Nevertheless, it is also obvious that the Hellenistic schools—with their almost evangelical insistence that happiness is available to practitioners in the immediacy of the "now"—take pride of place in Plotinus' short screed on the subject.[1] As French philosopher Pierre Hadot and

1 Hadot (1995, 217–237). Parts of this Introduction have been previously published in Layne (2019, 445–460).

others have noted,[2] both schools, Stoics and Epicureans, paradoxically suggested that one instant of happiness is equal to an eternity of happiness. For the Epicurean, "Infinite time and finite time contain equal pleasure, if one measures the limits of pleasure by reasoning [. . .]" (Epicurus, *Principle Doctrines* 19 = Diogenes Laertius, *Lives of the Eminent Philosophers* 10.145, 20, trans. Long and Sedley), while for the Stoic, "A good is not increased by the addition of time, but even if someone becomes prudent only for a moment, in respect of happiness he will in no way fall short of someone who employs virtue forever and lives his life blissfully in virtue" (Plutarch, *Common Conceptions* 1061f = *Stoicorum Veterum Fragmenta* III 54, trans. Long and Sedley). As Marcus Aurelius further extols, in *Meditations* II.14:

> Even if one's life is to last three thousand years or for that matter thirty thousand, bear in mind that no one ever parts with any other life than the one which he is now living, nor lives any other than that which he now parts. The longest life, then, and the shortest amount are but the same. For the present time is of equal duration for all, while that which we lose is not ours; consequently what is parted with is obviously a mere moment. No man

2 See particularly Linguiti (2016, 189–198).

> can part with either the past or the future. For how can a man be deprived of what he does not possess? These two things, then, must needs be remembered: the one, that all things from time everlasting have been cast in the same mold and repeated cycle after cycle, and so it makes no difference whether a man see the same things recur through a hundred or two hundred, or through eternity: the other, that the longest liver and the one whose time to die comes soonest, part with no more the one than the other. For it is but the present that a man can be deprived of, if, as is the fact, it is this alone that he has, and what he has not a man cannot part with (trans. Haines, modified).[3]

Overall, the Hellenistic schools suggested to followers that despite suffering and confusion, violence and death, change and turmoil, there is room for human happiness, be it absolutely unmixed pleasure (Epicureans) or a sense of belonging to the infinitely ordered cosmos (Stoics). Obviously, in an age of much discontent, these were attractive philosophical ways of life, so much so

---

3 See also *Med.*, IV 50 and 293.

that Plotinus would certainly need to respond to them and would be more in harmony with these schools over and against Aristotelian and Peripatetic conceptions of human flourishing, which, by contrast, required a lifetime to measure.[4] Like his Hellenistic counterparts, Plotinus would argue against Aristotle, emphasizing 1) that human well-being belongs to all in the immediacy of the present and 2) that one instant of well-being is equal to a lifetime. This agreement is indeed peculiar, particularly because one of the decisive differences between the Hellenistic schools and Plotinian Platonism is not merely Plotinus' rejection of a strict materialism (more will be said on this in the next section), but his adherence to the value of metaphysical theorizing over practical ethics. In other words, the Stoics and Epicureans are decisively more concerned with the question of how one ought to live—even at the expense (and sometimes in spite) of ontological, metaphysical, and psychological programmatics—while Plotinus' systematic ontology takes pride of place over his practical anxieties. Now, this ontological focus in the Platonist, however, does not mean that Plotinus dismissed or was less concerned with the particulars of living a moral life than the Hellenistic philosophers.[5] On the contrary, Plotinus

4 See Linguiti (2000).

5 See Dillon (1996) who argued that Plotinus' ethic does not offer much "practical guidance for the common man." Counter this view see Remes (2006, 1–23) and (2008, 213–238), Stern-Gillet (2009, 331–345) as well as Smith (1999, 335–344) and (2005, 65–72).

insisted on building a way of life from the top down. The question of human flourishing, in Plotinus' estimation, was less about securing an ethic, that is, advancing a prescriptive code of conduct, than showing how Platonic ontology fortified authentic well-being from its source, even if this meant abandoning commonplace ideas about the good life or even more lofty notions of the image of the virtuous sage-philosopher. As such, Plotinus will have much with which to disagree in the Stoic and Epicurean accounts of human happiness while still retaining the valorization of the present.

Admittedly, much of the ethical points of contrast between Plotinus and the Hellenistic schools (as well as Aristotle) can be found more broadly in the complementary treatise *Ennead* I.4 [46] *On Well-Being*. In this text Plotinus clearly separates human well-being from the life well-lived, emphasizing a contrasting way of life for an adherent to Plotinian Neoplatonism. Here, Plotinus asserts the need to identify well-being with the hypostatic level of *Nous* before he criticizes the identity of the good life with the rational life found in almost all of the competing schools. To some extent, Plotinus argues, this is true, but, unfortunately, none of the schools elevate the contemplative life to a level that can truly secure impassible well-being.[6] Individuals who reduce the world to the material,

6 See especially McGroarty (2006, 67–70, 175–176) as well as Ciapalo (1997, 489–498).

for example the Stoics and Epicureans, unfortunately cannot escape the fact that they would always feel the weight of their suffering even in their steadfast commitment to virtue. It may be mitigated through their forms of virtuous rational activity, but the prison of the body would always interrupt, always lurk like a shadow over human well-being. Plotinus' insistence on a transcendent soul in contact or united to *Nous* ultimately clarifies *how* well-being is still possible even when one is in physical distress. As intelligible rather than corporeal, intellectual activity is a completely separable and untouched form of life, essentially other than the life of the body, therein more adeptly securing human well-being regardless of one's physical and external circumstances. In other words, despite their arguments to the contrary, the Epicurean and the Stoic cannot defend against the vicissitudes of human fortune, as they are condemned to the material and, as such, will always be affected by the material. Much of the same, or more, could be said of Aristotle insofar as he had no problem subjecting human well-being to the relative conditions with which humans find themselves.

While much of these subjects saturate I.5 [36], the earlier of the two texts concerned with the life of the *eudaimōn*, this much shorter treatise has some unique features distinguishing it from the goals of I.4 [46], which we can introduce here. First, Plotinus repeatedly emphasizes that the source of human well-being is a certain inner disposition (*diathesis*) of the soul. As we shall see, this disposition is not a passive state[7] but is rather the active source of our life, the true life at the hypostatic level of *Nous*—a point which this treatise shares with I.4, but here is markedly described as a disposition, allowing for a new point of contrast with the competing Aristotelian and Stoic conceptions of disposition and habit (*hexis*).[8] For Plotinus this inner disposition is the ground of authentic desire, for a life at rest in the eternal embrace of *Nous*—a desire that is and can only be sated in the present moment. Indeed, perhaps the most poignant point of I.5 is the fact that insofar as this disposition resides in *Nous* Plotinus is able to clarify the difference between a temporal and eternal life, denying well-being to the former and securing it as a hallmark of the latter. Interestingly, this discussion of eternity and time leads Plotinus to analyze repeatedly the role memory has for the good life, appealing to distinctions between the recollection of the Forms, characteristic of intellectual life, and embodied memories, stemming from a life lived as a composite of body and soul. Overall, the present moment becomes the site of eternal life wherein one needs neither memory of the past nor hope for an ameliorated future insofar as the present always bears within it an appropriate limit and border. The present moment, as the site of eternal life, needs nothing, wants for

7 See Stamatellos (2016, 130).

8 See Gerson (1994, 199).

nothing and, as such, is complete. Strikingly, this account of the perfection of the present follows Aristotle's and Epicurean analyses of complete pleasure, assisting Plotinus in unpacking and elevating these theories to the plane of *Nous*, while also allowing the Platonist to critique the role of pleasure in the good life. Finally, Plotinus concludes with one of his more challenging ethical suppositions, namely, that virtue is not the source of the good life, that is, being good may result in being virtuous (see I.2.7, 10–11) but well-being is not caused by the virtuous life. Rather, the contemplative life, residing in the eternal, is the true cause of our well-being. Again, Plotinus insists it is the inner disposition, our life at the level of *Nous*, which is the source of human virtue and "noble actions" and so he stresses at the end of the treatise that we safeguard this disposition above all else. The two earlier treatises *On Virtue* I.2 [19] and *On Dialectic* I.3 [20] are therein complementary to Plotinus' project. Like I.5 they are concerned with the ethical implications of Plotinus' ontological shift to the value of one's internal disposition marking the soul's true life as well as with assisting practitioners in rethinking the nature of virtue and the import of the contemplative life. In the end, this contemplative life, our well-being, is not concerned with this world, but concentrated on the inner ascent to another, an inner ascent toward the reality of our selves, which is available to us *all* right now.

1. The Inner Disposition of the Soul

Stoic and Epicurean philosophies were markedly materialistic, reducing everything to the corporeal, thereby situating the good *in*, rather than outside of, the sensible world. For these Hellenistic schools there is nothing but the sensible, nothing but corporeality. Contrariwise, Plotinus locates the good in the transcendent life of the eternal, which is located in the *reality* of the present that gives human beings access to what is other than the corporeal, that which is, markedly, the cause of the corporeal without itself being subsumed into the corporeal. To summarize at the outset, in opposition to the Stoic and Epicurean insistence on human finitude and their somatic reductionism, the Neoplatonist, in the spirit of Socrates' remarks in the *Theaetetus*, heralded the idea that human happiness lay in becoming, as much as is possible, divine.[9] Put differently,

9 See *Theaetetus* 175e–176b. Cf. *Phaedrus* 237a–b, *Symposium* 220d, *Phaedo* 117c. For further references to the Platonic concept of "becoming like god" see also *Republic* 613b1 and *Timaeus* 90d. See I.2 [19] 6, 2–3 for this familiar refrain in Plotinus' ethics. Of course, the Stoics, Epicureans, and Aristotle would all in some sense valorize and extol the importance of becoming god-like for achieving happiness but ultimately all, for Plotinus, would have a limited understanding of that likeness, e.g. the Stoic and Epicurean god is wholly corporeal (see Alexander, *On Mixture* 225, 1–2 = *Stoicorum Veterum Fragmenta* II 310 and Lucretius, *On the Nature of Things*, V 146–55), while Aristotle's god is, in Plotinus' estimation, an empty thought thinking itself, neither turned outward to the world nor beyond toward its origin in that which is unity itself, the

well-being depends on transcending the sensible and uniting/identifying with that which causes and sustains being, the incorporeal ground of all life. As Plotinus urges us:

> II.3.9, 19–33
> "[. . .] we must fly from here" [*Theaetetus* 176a8–b1] and "separate" [*Phaedo* 67c6] ourselves from our accretions [*Republic* 611d4] and not be the ensouled composite body, in which the nature of the body, which has received a trace of the soul, is more in command, since the life common to body and soul belongs more to the body. For everything that belongs to this common life is related to the body. But to the other soul that is outside the body belongs the motion to the higher world and to what is beautiful and what is divine, of which no one is master. Either one makes use of it in order to be it oneself and, having withdrawn from the sensible world,

One or the Good. See *Nicomachean Ethics* 1177b26–1178a8 for Aristotle's powerful account of the necessity for human beings to become like the divine as far as possible. Cf. 1166a22–23, 1168b31–33. See also Seneca, *Epistles* 92. 30: "But he in whose body virtue dwells, and spirit is present, is equal to the Gods, and, mindful of his origin, strives to return there. No man does wrong in attempting to regain the heights from which he once came down. And why should you not believe that something of divinity exists in one who is part of God."

> to live by it; or else, if one comes to be bereft of this soul, one lives in the domain of fate [. . .] (trans. Gerson, slightly adapted).[10]

Here, we see Plotinus' complex psychology, where he roundly distinguishes his theory from the Epicurean and Stoic reduction of soul to body[11] as well as Aristotle's arguments that identify the soul with the *entelecheia* of the body.[12] In contrast to both the Hellenistic somatic commitment and the Aristotelian psychic bondage to the body, Plotinus warns of such false identifications, insisting that there is something other than the embodied soul, that is, a soul whose primary purpose would be to utilize, activate, and rule the body. Beyond this, there

10 All translations of the *Enneads* that are not my own are from Gerson (2018). Any adaptations will be noted. The edition used is Henry and Schwyzer (1982).

11 For the Epicurean collapse of the soul into corporeality see *Letter to Herodotus* 67 = Diogenes Laertius, *Lives of the Eminent Philosophers* 10 63: "Consequently those who say that the soul is incorporeal are talking nonsense. For if it were like that it would be unable to act or be acted upon in any way [. . .]" (trans. Long and Sedley). Cf. Lucretius, *On the Nature of Things* III 136–176, 624–633. For the Stoic agreement see Seneca *Epistles* 106.2 = *SVF* 3 84.73: "For the soul, too, is corporeal. *Ergo*, man's good is corporeal, since man himself is corporeal." Cf. Nemesius 78, 7–79, 2 = *SVF* I 518 and 81, 6–10 = *SVF* II 790.

12 In other words, the soul and the body are not two separable substances but the "the soul is that by which we live, perceive and have understanding primarily" (*De Anima* 414a12–13 and, again, 412a26–27). Cf. also *Metaphysics* 1035b14–16; 1043a29–1043b4.

is the ground of one's being, life, and intellect, the "true self" or the intellectual self, the active agent contemplating the offspring of the Good, that is, reality and form, and, in so doing, understanding what it itself actually *is*. This intelligible soul, to be clear, is not the modern "I," a conscious "ego," for Plotinus, but rather, as emphasized in I.5 Chapters 1 and 10, it is the active inner disposition *(diathesis)* of the soul, a disposition that constitutes our movement or desire toward absolutely real being.[13] Strikingly, this disposition constitutes the soul's relation with *Nous*, therein securing its life as that which is more than a temporal creature, haphazardly pushed around by

13 To be sure, Plotinus' use of *diathesis* appears to be inconsistent, sometimes appearing as a passive state, while *hexis* is contrastingly the more active state (VI.3.19.31–32). See Stamatellos (2015, 132). Nevertheless, there is marked consistency in Plotinus' use of *diathesis* once we recognize he believes that dispositions vary depending on the type of life to which one is appealing. For further references to the intellectual disposition of the soul see I.2.3, 19; I.6.5, 4, and 16; III.7.11, VI.7.30, 18–23. On the permanence of a disposition, i.e., all disposition whether it be the disposition to intellect for the human soul or toward sensible life for the animal (or the human who identifies with the sensual, see below), see VI.1.11, 1–7. Cf. IV.3.12, 38; IV.3.13, 3; IV.3.24, 7; IV.4.45, 3. On the disposition of the soul that leads downward, i.e., somatic dispositions, see VI.3.16, 26 and IV.4.28, 29 or its dual disposition that makes the original disposition toward *Nous* faint, see VI.7.5, 13–18. Cf. III.5.7, 45. For further references to this disposition which seems to be connected to our constitutive desires see the Commentary, esp. Chapters 1, 7, and 10. See Marsola (2016, 82–95) for a discussion of this passage and the identification of the three types of attitude ascending from the sensible to the intelligible.

atoms in the void (Epicureans) or unbending Fate (Stoics). Illustrating the various levels of corporeal commitment that orient the Epicurean and Stoic way of life, particularly their view of reason as either a hedonist calculus or the *logos* at the service of sensibility,[14] Plotinus poetically appeals, in V.9.1, 8–13, to the intellectual disposition of those who ascend to an altogether different vantage point:

> Those [the Epicureans], at least, who pretend that they are just being rational, lay this down as wisdom, like heavy birds who, taking in a lot from the earth, and being weighed down by it, are unable to fly high even though they are naturally equipped with wings. Others

14 As McGroarty (2006, 67) succinctly comments on Plotinus' lukewarm acceptance of the Stoic valorization of reason in his analysis of *Enneads* I.4.33: "Plotinus concedes that the Stoics are at least in the right area when they identify the rational life with *eudaimonia*. In his own view (outlined in chapters 3 and 4), *eudaimonia* is possible only for the possessors of reason, since the first step in the return to *Nous* is the process of dialectic. See *Enneads* I.3 in general. The Stoics will be criticized (below) for not explaining satisfactorily why this is so. The Stoic *logos* is ultimately based on sensory knowledge while Plotinus' *eudaimonia* is guided by principles from *Nous*. Quite often throughout [I.4] the Stoics and Plotinus appear, *prima facie*, to be in agreement, but differing metaphysical frameworks allow Plotinus to provide explanations for his assertions, based on a many-layered ontology, and at the same time to criticize the Stoics because of their one-level material reality." For confirmation that the Stoic use of reason was at the service of the empirical see Epictetus, *Discourses* 1 20, 5–6.

> [the Stoics] are furnished with the ability to ascend a little from things here below by the better part of their soul moving them from that which is pleasurable to that which is more beautiful. But, having nowhere to plant themselves, they are unable to see above, and are brought down to a nominal virtue concerned with their own actions and "choices" made of those things here below from which they first tried to elevate themselves. But there is a third type of divine human being who, with superior power and sharp-sightedness, saw as if by a piercing vision, the glory up above and raised itself to the intelligible world, in a way, beyond the clouds and the obscurity of the sensible world and remained in the intelligible world looking down on all the things here. They were delighted by being in a true and familiar place, as if after much wandering a human being arrived in his well-governed fatherland. What, then, is this place? And how might one reach it? One who is a lover by nature and from the start really has the *disposition* of a philosopher might reach it [. . .].

In other words, the Epicurean and Stoic appeal to reason and its corresponding virtue is to be sharply contrasted with the "superior power and sharp-sightedness" of the elevated philosopher who remains "in the intelligible world looking down on all the things here" (V.9.1, 17–18).[15] So, despite agreeing with the Stoic and even Aristotelian valorization of intellectual contemplation as the true and divine work or function of the human being,[16] Plotinus'

---

15 See I.4.13, 4–15 where Plotinus makes this clear in his criticism of Epicurean philosophy which contradictorily believes it can escape the pain of the body via their hedonistically oriented rational practices: "As for theoretical activities, those that are concerned with particulars might be impeded, for example, those that require enquiries and investigations. But 'the greatest study' [cf. *Republic* 505a2] is always available to the virtuous and always with him, and all the more so even if he were inside what is called 'the bull of Phalaris,' which, no matter how many times it is claimed to be 'pleasurable,' is hardly so. For according to them, that which says this is that which is in pain, whereas according to us, that which is in pain is one thing, but that which accompanies this is another, and even if he by necessity accompanies it, he would not be bereft of the vision of the universal Good." Cf. Seneca, *Moral Letters to Lucilius* 66. 18 and Cicero, *Tusculan Disputations* 2. 17. The Bull of Phalaris was noted to be an oven, heated to interminable degrees in which prisoners were torturously baked. See Linguiti (2016, 192–194). Cf. *Nicomachean Ethics* 7 13 1153b19–21 where Aristotle rejects, as nonsense, the possibility of human happiness even under extreme torture.

16 For Aristotle see *Nicomachean Ethics* 1106a23–24, 1175b30–1176b12, and 1177a16–18. Cf. *Metaphysics* 1072b13–1694. For the Stoics see Seneca *Epistles* 76. 9 = fr. 200a *SVF* 3: "What quality is best in man? It is reason; by virtue of reason he surpasses the animals, and is surpassed only by the Gods. Perfect reason is therefore the good peculiar to man; all other qualities he shares in some degree with animals and plants. . . Hence, if everything is praiseworthy and has arrived at the end intended by its nature,

system demands a complete stripping of the soul down to its fundamental and simple core, whereby our thoughts are no longer oriented to the things of this world, not because we are merely indifferent to the trappings of this world, as the Stoic would demand, but because we no longer identify with such things. Rather, we will identify with our inner disposition oriented to the divine:

> IV.7.10, 30–40
> Examine [the soul] by actually subtracting that element [i.e. that which looks to externals], or rather subtract himself and then look, and he will come to believe that he is immortal, when he contemplates himself on the intelligible level and as having come into a pure world. For he will see an intellect viewing no sensible, nor any of mortal things here, but grasping with the everlasting aspect of itself the everlasting reality, all the contents of the intelligible world, a world itself intelligible and suffused with light, beaming illuminated by the truth radiating from the Good, which beams its truth upon all the intelligibles; so

when it has brought its peculiar good to perfection, and if man's peculiar good is reason, then if a man has brought his reason to perfection, he is praiseworthy and has reached the end suited to his nature." See also Cicero *De finibus* 3.7.23; Epictetus *Discourses* I 16, 21 or *Encheiridon* 24 4.

> that often it should occur to him that this is indeed well said: "Hail, I am to you as an immortal god!"—as he ascends to the divine, and focuses his attention on the sameness he has to it.

Overall, for Plotinus this disposition is the true life of the soul, the noetic life that ascends to contemplate the radiations of the Good. As McGroarty (2006) and Ciapalo (1997) observe in their respective examinations of I.4,[17] this noetic life is not the mere having of life, which is what takes place at the level of the corporeal, but it is life in its eternal propriety. Plotinus further extols the difference between absolute and relative life, ultimately reserving well-being to the former:

> I.4.3, 25–40
> If, then, living well belongs to something living fully—meaning to something which is in no way deficient of life—well-being will belong only to one living fully, for the best will belong to this, if indeed that which is really best in life, that is, the perfect life, is something that exists. For in this way, the goodness that exists in happiness would not be something superadded nor will something else from

17 Ciapalo (2006, 40).

> somewhere else provide the substrate for its being good. [. . .] It has been said many times that the perfect *Life* and the true and real *Life* is in that intellectual nature and that the other sorts of life are imperfect and reflections of life and do not exist perfectly or purely, and are no more lives than the opposite of this. And now let it be said summarily that so long as all living beings are from one source and they do not have life in the same way that it does, it is necessary that the source is the primary *Life*, that is, the most perfect *Life* (trans. Gerson with slight adaptations).

In short, all other forms of life are but pale reflections of *Life* itself. Nevertheless, even in this mundane state, intelligible *Life* remains an essential disposition of the human soul, marking it with an uncanny but constitutive possibility to exist and live on a higher ontological plane than other living beings—an argument that Plotinus is also at pains to make in I.5.[18] Indeed, beyond the arguments

18 I.4 is markedly concerned with differentiating *eudaimonia* from living well (τὸ εὖ ζῆν), i.e., the simple fulfillment of one's end or *telos*, so as to reserve the former to humanity as Ciapolo (1997) and McGroarty (2006) explore. See Aristotle, *Nicomachean Ethics* 1095a19–20 as well as 1098b20–21 and for the Stoics and Epicureans see *SVF* 3 7 and 65. For whether Aristotle is subject to these criticisms by Plotinus see Ciapalo (1987) as well as McGroarty (2006, 46–48). I.5 in contrast to I.4 shares little of this concern on

of I.4, mostly concerned with securing the singularity of *eudaimonia* for an ontological domain reserved for human beings, the main purpose of I.5 is to demarcate this absolute form of *Life* with the disposition of the soul that orients itself toward Intellect. One need only turn inward, discovering the shared life toward which the soul inclines us and toward which it is already pre-disposed—a life shared not with the body but the transcendent intellect.

2. Eternal vs. Temporal Life

Obviously, I.5 and Plotinus' conception of human well-being is dependent upon his conception of time and eternity, particularly III.7, insofar as the demarcation between time and eternity results from his distinction between the life of soul and the *Life* of *Nous*. This identity radically breaks with both the Epicurean and Stoic conceptions of time. For the Epicureans, time as an accident of bodies "does not exist *per se*" (Lucretius, *On the Nature of Things* I.456)[19] and for the Stoics time's reality is precariously

safeguarding a particular form of life to humanity but still depends substantially on this elevated understanding of Life.

19 Cf. Epicurus, *Letter to Herodotus* 72; Sextus Empiricus, *Against the Professors* 10, 226 as well as Cicero, *On the Nature of the Gods* I 22 where it is argued that despite not existing *per se*, there was never a time that time did not exist: "But there has been a certain eternity from infinite time past, which was not measured by any bounding of times, but whose extent can be understood, because it

classified as one of the four species of incorporeals, that is, *lekta* or sayables.[20] As Proclus observed, "[The Stoics] regard [time] as subsisting merely in accordance with thought, something feeble and close to Not-Being (for time was one among the incorporeal things according to them —things which were of course disdained by them as lacking causal efficacy and as 'not beings' which subsist merely in thought)" (*Commentary on Plato's Timaeus* III.95, 11–14 trans. Baltzly = *SVF* 2 521). As most observe, Plotinus' understanding of time, by contrast, secures for it a more substantial kind of reality than the Epicurean and Stoic conceptions would allow. Due to this Plotinus can permit an ontological reformulation of the value of the present moment, a reformulation that grounds the value of the present not in an ethical prescription or commandment but in the metaphysical ascent of the soul. To unpack a bit more, as most scholars observe, Plotinus' understanding of time is heavily indebted to his reading of Plato's *Timaeus* in which time is defined as the "moving image of eternity."[21] Utilizing this definition, Plotinus conceives of time as the *life* of the soul, while eternity is the *Life* of that which always "is."[22] In opposition to time,

is unthinkable that there should have been some time at which there was no time."

20 See Sextus Empiricus, *Against the Professors* 10, 218.

21 *Timaeus* 37d.

22 See Sorabji (1083, 138) who notes the influence of Philo, *On the Change of Names* 47, 267.

eternity is defined as *Life simpliciter,* without otherness, and, as such, is not an "intellection or life that goes from one thing to another, but a state of stability and constant lack of extension; when you have seen all this you have seen eternity" (III.7.3, 12–15). Plotinus continues:

> III.7.3, 15–23
> It is when you have seen life abiding forever in the identical state and possessing everything in its presence, not now this, again something else, but all at once, and not now some things, now others, but partless perfection, it is just as in a point where all things are together and none of them ever flows forth but remains in identity in itself and never changes, being always in the present because nothing of it has slipped away or again will come to be, but it is what it is.

Here, we should clarify a few important issues in Plotinus' thinking on eternity. First, eternity is not to be equated with the intelligible realm, neither as a whole nor as a part. Eternity is neither the being of the whole nor a part of the whole because it is rather the *Life* of the whole. As Plotinus says, "Eternity is not the substrate, but something which, as it were, shines out from the substrate itself" (III.7.3, 25–26). As Andrew Smith described it, "[Eternity] is 'around' (*peri*) Being and is seen *in* it. It manifests itself *from* Being, like light caused by something else, dependent on and attached to its cause but different from it."[23] In short, Plotinus is foreshadowing or laying the groundwork for the later Neoplatonic understanding of the triad of Being, Life, and Intellect, whereby Life/Eternity is the processive power of inchoate Being, the activity of Being in coming to think or understand itself as a procession from the One/Good. To explain in the terms of the later Platonists, life is the activity of the *intelligible* in contemplation of itself as object, the *intellective*, and, as such, life is the *intelligible-intellective* or that which substantiates the isomorphic relation between the subject and object of thought. It is the self-kinetic movement of Being in thinking itself that is non-successive; otherwise it would have parts that were truly distinct and not unified.[24] The *Life* of eternity is the uncanny movement of Being that constitutes authentic continuity and connection between the subject and object(s) of thought, establishing or revealing the intelligible realm as a whole and complete in its perfect contemplation of its origin, the One. Notably, Plotinus will call eternity the disposition and nature of Intellect (III.7.4, 44: *diathesis, physis*)[25]—a

23 Smith (1996, 201). See also Viglas (2006).

24 See Emilsson (2007, 124–175) and Perl (2006, 1–26).

25 Contra see I.2.3, 23–32 where it is said that the divine do not have dispositions. I take this to be an ambiguity that results from the fact

disposition/nature that, as we have already seen, we share despite our lower temporal life, the life the soul lives in coming to reproduce the continuity and perfection of eternity in time.

Time, then, in contrast to eternity, is "the life of soul in its changing motion from one way of life to another" (III.7.11, 43–44) and "as an image of eternity" it is the unfolding or succession of being versus the complete and immediate veracity of being. Time "runs around" its center, "dropping some things and picking up others. For at the level of Soul, thoughts are always changing; now it thinks of Socrates, now a horse—always some particular being—whereas Intellect just is everything" (V.I.4, 15–21).[26] Eternity is the life of absolute being, undivided and unextended. Time, however, is the life of the soul that moves, lives, and thinks successively from one distinct moment to another, never truly possessing or uniting with the object of its thought, absolutely real being, or the good from which it has sprung. Time can do no more than order things in a sequence that mirrors the

that for Plotinus a disposition is not a passive state but an inclination, a kind of built-in pre-disposed desire which is absolutely active at the level of intellect and so its life, its inclining, is not needy. The use of disposition in this passage then is an attempt to appeal to eternity as a perfect inclining toward Being, an absolute disposition. See also VI.6.6, 38 for Plotinus' appeal to disposition to explain Intellect's activity toward Justice.

26 See Majumdar (2007).

continuity or connection binding the world of the intelligible. Plotinus writes that the "extension of time means the dispersal of a single present" and so soul must think, be and live in succession, in parts.[27] It contemplates not all at once as eternity does, but only incrementally and always incompletely.[28] It is "always on the way to being"; it becomes but never "is" insofar as its being or life must be made manifest in time. The life of the soul, be it the rational soul or the body-soul composite, is a constant seeking versus a having of being, an always anticipatory heralding of that which it hopes to be, namely, absolute being as opposed to temporal being. In the soul's longing for being, it projects itself into the future, always desiring eternal versus temporal life, eager to achieve well-being or true being for always. It is this transcendent or divine life of intellect that the soul truly desires, not its own temporal life that never truly "is." In contrast, Plotinus believes that "the desire (*ephesis*) [of the soul] is for that which is better than itself, by which, when it arrives, the soul is satisfied and at rest, and this is really the life that is willed"[29] (I.4.6, 17–19). Further, describing the soul's desire for absolute life not found in time but only in eternity, Plotinus valorizes the present moment, writing:

27 I.5.7, 14–15.

28 See Baracat (2013, 25–42).

29 See Gerson (2012).

> I.5.2, 9–15
> Then desire, attaining its end, has attained that which is present and always that which is present and seeks to have well-being while it exists. So the desire for life, as it seeks existence, is of the present, if existence is in the present. And even if the desire were for the future and what comes next, yet it wishes for what it has and is, not what is gone or what will come, but what already is, for this to exist, not seeking the forever, but for the already present to exist now (trans. Layne).

Overall, for Plotinus, time tempts the human soul into a sea of dispersion, into a never-ending series of discrete "nows" admitting of destruction, a future "no longer." Insofar as we desire well-being and well-being is identified with absolutely real being, Plotinus argues that "[well-being] should not be counted by time, but eternity, for this is neither more nor less nor any length, but is a 'this,' unextended and not existent in time" (I.5.7, 25–30). Put otherwise, we do not come into contact with real being in the past or the future, but only right now, as active intellectual contemplation occurs in the indivisible immediacy of the present, in an immediacy that always "is."[30]

30 For Proclus' complementary but also contrasting theory of the

3. Memory

The disposition of the soul appealed to in I.5 as inclined toward eternal life rather than temporal life, demands that Plotinus rethink the role of memory for human well-being. Insofar as eternal life is neither concerned for the past nor inclined toward the future but always "is," eternal life has no use for the faculty of memory. In general, for Plotinus "memory, even if it is of the best things, is itself not one of the best things" (IV.4.4, 7–8) and, as such, is not to be incorporated, as it was for the Epicurean, into human well-being.[31] Interestingly and perhaps paradoxically, the Epicureans held fast to the idea that memory could markedly improve well-being insofar as, unlike the body that perceives only present pleasure, "the mind perceives both the present pleasure, along with the body, and foresees the one that is coming without allowing the past one to flow away. Hence the wise man will always have a constant supply of tight-knit pleasures, since the anticipation of pleasures hoped for is united with the recollection of

relationship between the human soul's temporal life and one's well-being see Layne (2019).

31 See IV.4.4, 12–15 and IV.3.32, 13–19 for examples how somatic memory is a descent or a failing to differentiate between what one is and what one has. For Plotinus' direct response to the Epicurean theory that memory of the past contributes to happiness see Commentary on Chapter 8.

those already experienced" (Cicero, *Tusculan Disputations* 5. 95, trans. Long and Sedley).

In contrast to this insistence that the present moment can be saturated with the bundling of past, present, and future pleasure, Plotinus will insist that well-being will be a returning to that which has no need of memory, particularly memories of past events, feelings or actions, namely, the somatic memory of the body-soul composite. Here, we should recall that at the level of *Nous* there is no extension or division and so no past or experience of any kind to be recalled. Memory, ultimately, arises when the soul has fallen, displaced from the perfection of the life above. Yet, due to the inner intellectual disposition that unites the soul to *Nous*, human beings have a kind of unconscious memory of the intelligible world, which, through activities like dialectic, can be recollected. In short, throughout I.5 Plotinus plays with this ambiguity in his theory of memory, suggesting that memory of the Beautiful has something to do with human well-being while memory of beautiful things does not. The former appeals to recollection, while the latter is explicitly characterized as that which should be forgotten.[32] This latter

32 For Platonic references to recollection see *Phaedo* 73a–76d, *Phaedrus* 249e–250a, *Meno* 85d, *Philebus* 33c–34c. In fact, the *Phaedrus,* to my mind, seems to be the background for Plotinus' view of a dual memory in Platonism insofar as in this text Plato depicts the vulgarity of recalling things like speeches from things like written texts, e.g. Lysias or the myth of Theuth, as it causes us to

form of memory occurs in time and is the result of the soul's descent into becoming, its wanton desire for individuality that must be shed if one is to ascend and return to the intelligible (IV.4.5, 11–13). In I.5 Plotinus refers to the latter of the two forms of memory, that is, somatic, experiential memories, when emphasizing that memory does not participate in human well-being.[33] Memories are not to be trusted, because they are not absolutely real insofar as they are tied to the experience of the body. Rather, only the recollection of that which is perfect and outside of all temporality, meaning Form, allows us to rekindle our connection to the eternal. In this, Plotinus reinforces the value of a kind of forgetting that marks the life of the *eudaimōn*: "Indeed, to the extent that [the higher soul] strives upwards, it forgets more things—unless perhaps all its life even in the sensible world was somehow such that it has memories only of better things. In this connection, the remark about 'standing apart from human concerns' [*Phaedrus* 249c8–d1] is most apt; this necessarily comprises memory, too" (IV.3.32, 13–19).

become forgetful of the ideas as such. This "aid to memory" (which is actually an aid to forgetting) is contrasted with the recollection of the divine inspired by one's beloved and enacted in the ascent of the soul through dialectic.

33 See Blumenthal (1971, 95–99), Warren (1965, 252–260), Gerson (1994, 180–183) and King (2009) for more information on the dual role of memory in Plotinus and for the relevant debates in scholarship regarding this issue.

4. Pleasure

Ultimately, the good life, insofar as it resembles or is identical to the *Life* of *Nous*, will be self-contained. It has an appropriate limit, the present moment, and thus does not need the memories of the past or hopes for the future. Indeed, the perfect limit of the present, the "time" which needs not more time, is in I.5 interestingly and repeatedly tied to Epicurean and Aristotelian concepts of pleasure.[34] In this treatise Plotinus follows Aristotle's account of pleasure, whereby pleasure results from the unimpeded activity of our natural state[35] and the similar Epicurean insistence that pleasure has a limit that cannot be increased but only qualitatively altered.[36] Plotinus incorporates both these ideas into his model of human well-being:

---

34 See Van Riel (2000, 94–120) for the most comprehensive account of Plotinus' concept of pleasure and his use of both Aristotelian and Epicurean theories of pleasure in his view of well-being as well as the ambiguities surrounding whether or not Plotinus accepted a kind of Stoic joy at the highest levels of human well-being.

35 Aristotle, *Nicomachean Ethics* VII 13, 1153a10–15; X 4, 1174b23–26; X 4, 1174b31–33.

36 Epicurus, *Principle Doctrines* 3 and 18; Cicero, *De finibus* I 38. Cf. Linguiti (2016, 195). For the Platonic conception of pleasure as unlimited see *Philebus* 24e–28a, 64–66d while Aristotle's opposing remarks can be found in *Nicomachean Ethics* 1173a15–17. See Epicurus, *Principle Doctrines* 20 where the pleasures of the flesh are described as unlimited and therein insatiable while the pleasures of the mind are limited and therein perfect. See also Linguiti (2016, 197) for a concise explanation of Epicurean indebtedness to the Aristotelian conception of pleasure.

> I.5.3–4
> 3. What, then, about [the phrase] "He has been happier for more time and for more time he saw the same thing with his eyes"? Well, if he saw more accurately with more [time], then time would have produced something more for him. But if he saw to the same degree all along, then, in seeing once, he has just as much [as the other].
>
> 4. But, [one might argue], the other man was pleased for a longer time. But it would not be correct to count this toward well-being. And if someone were to characterize pleasure as *unhindered activity*, he is saying the same as what we are aiming at. And in any case this greater pleasure only ever has what is present; its past pleasure has gone (trans. and emphasis are my own).

Plotinus therein argues in affinity with the Epicurean and the Stoic positions that present well-being is equivalent to an infinite amount of happiness in time, reminding his readers that well-being is not a mere feeling or passive state of the soul. Rather, to echo but also explicitly to overturn

Aristotle, it is an unhindered *activity* of the soul[37]; it is the soul in its *actuality*—again, a state or disposition that is not merely psychic but intellectual. While explicitly concerned with the question of whether this activity or disposition has a corresponding pleasure, as Aristotle would argue, Plotinus writes:

> VI.7.30, 18–23
> . . . since there must be something that follows or accompanies all activity, disposition, and life—on the one hand, insofar as [sensual pleasure] is a hindrance to this life proceeding naturally, since something of the contrary is mixed with it, which does not allow its life to be, whereas, on the other hand, the act in the other life is "pure and clean"; and life shines out in its disposition—those who, having claimed that the state we have been discussing, which belongs to intellect, and is more worthy of being welcomed with joy, and most worthy of being chosen, say intellect is mixed with pleasure, do this due to a lack of a proper designation.

37 I.5.4, 4. Cf. Aristotle, *Nicomachean Ethics* 1153b10–12.

In short, Plotinus adapts theories such as Epicurean katastematic pleasure, that is, static pleasure unmixed with pain, and Aristotle's concept of pleasure as that which follows from the unhindered activity of the soul, into his Platonic metaphysical schema by situating well-being (as opposed to pleasure) into the transcendent vision of the Forms, complete and perfect, and readily available in the present. This vision, in its perfection, has an absolute limit that never requires more. There is no pleasure as such at this level, for Plotinus, but, rather, a kind of "glad-tiding" that accompanies unity with the intelligible (see also VI.7.30, 30), that some mistakenly refer to as pleasure (as Plato himself did, much to Plotinus' chagrin [cf. *Philebus* 63d–64a]).[38] Overall, once the soul has achieved the intellectual vision that constitutes its actuality, it does not require any addition and so does not require more time. Appealing to the Epicurean notion of the limits of pleasure, Plotinus emphasizes that "one ought not speak in general of that as 'more,' reckoning the no-longer with what is. What concerns well-being has a border and a limit and is always identical."[39] Insofar as one would measure the complete or absolute by an infinite sequence of partiality that constitutes the corporeal and

38 See Van Riel (2000, 107–117) for Plotinus' attempt to harmonize his understanding of pleasure with Plato's seeming contradiction regarding the importance of pleasure for the good life laid out in the *Philebus*.

39 I.5.6, 17–20.

temporal world, an unlimited amount of time would still only be an always-on-the-way-to-being, a sort of promissory note never to be repaid, a wanton, libidinal yearning that can never quite grasp the object of its desire. In other words, more time, regardless of its length, would be of no more worth than the fullness of the unextended present, wherein we discover the boundary or limit, the absolute being, of human well-being: the intellectual soul in quiet contemplation of reality and its origin.

4. The Self-Sufficiency of the Inner Disposition: Contemplative vs. Practical Life

The self-sufficiency of contemplation, of the limit of well-being in the perfect and perfecting eternal life of *Nous*, thereby comes to draw out the largest ethical consequence of Plotinus' I.5, that is, the priority of the intellectual life over practical virtue. As he insists:

> I.5.10, 10–23
> [. . .] it is possible to become happy without actions, and to be not less but more so than the person of accomplishments. Then, actions do not offer up well-being out of themselves but one's dispositions are that which make actions beautiful. The practically wise enjoys the fruits of the good even from his actions,

> not because he acts, nor from the circumstances, but from out of that which he has. [. . .] To place well-being in the actions is to situate it outside of virtue and the soul. For the activity of the soul is in thought and being active within.

Markedly, Plotinus is keen to stress that beautiful actions are the result of one's inner intellectual disposition. Contra Aristotle and the Stoics, well-being is not a habit we accrue, not a way of life bent on performing "beautiful actions," but a self-reflexive journey of discovering the beautiful itself from within oneself. Overall, for Plotinus, practical virtue is too dependent upon the external world. As he emphasizes in VI.8.5, it is not really "up to us."[40]

> What is, then, up to virtue itself, as a habit or disposition? Should we not say it comes to order the badly disposed soul, by bringing measure to affect states and desires? How, then, will we say being good and "virtue without master" are up to us? In fact, insofar as it is willed and chosen. Or, because, when it has come about in us, it constitutes freedom and the "up to us," and does not permit us still to be slaves of what we were slaves to before. If,

40 See Eliasson (2008).

> then, virtue is in a way another intellect and a habit which makes the soul rational, then again being up to us does not belong to us in action, but to intellect detached from actions.

Remarkably, what we find in this passage is an acknowledgement that virtue, as commonly understood, is a necessitated action, an ordering or restoring of the body-soul composite, of the soul badly disposed because rather than being inclined toward itself it is turned toward what is alien to it. Beyond the civic virtues there are also the purgative virtues,[41] for Plotinus, but these, too, despite fostering ascent, insofar as they attempt to purify the soul from the body, are not divine activity proper. In other words, purgative virtue is still reliant on or defined by its relationship to this world (cf. I.2.6). In the end, virtue is not part of the intelligible: "Virtue belongs to soul, not to Intellect which transcends it" (I.2.5, 30–31; Cf. I.2.1, 18–22 and 45–51). Nevertheless, Plotinus still retains the vocabulary of virtue to describe the complete ascent to the intelligible and, in this, he transforms the Aristotelian conception of habit/disposition. It is this inner intellectual disposition, what he refers to as habit in VI.8.5, which

41 For more on the hierarchy of the virtues in Plotinus see Dillon (1983, 92–105) and Baltzly (2004, 297–321). See also Finamore (2012, 113–132).

is a kind of transcendent "virtue" in us, acting as the lodestone for all particular virtue. Identifying with one's noetic disposition is ultimately what makes all actions intelligible as virtuous or beautiful, therein evidencing why "intellect detached from actions" is more valuable in Plotinus' estimation. Like heat emanating from the sun, the inner disposition of the soul inclined toward the intelligible overflows and penetrates all that is beautiful and virtuous below. In this emphasis on the value of one's inner disposition it becomes clearer why Plotinus rejects the Aristotelian demand that human well-being be measured by the "complete life," because for Plotinus "one swallow will make a spring," so to speak. In other words, well-being is not to be measured by duration or the counting/adding up of all of one's good deeds or even a lifetime of exhibiting contemplative virtue wrapped up in the goings-on of the embodied life. Rather, it is coming to identify with the life of intellect, the inner disposition that secures psychic transcendence, which Plotinus describes as complete and measured by the life of eternity rather than by time—a well-being available right now and for always.

Note on the Greek Text

LINE NUMBERS IN THE TRANSLATION are approximate and do not always match the original Greek text. Since the commentary follows the sequence of the English translation, there may sometimes be a slight discrepancy in the ordering.

The Greek text adopted is that of the Oxford edition, that is, the *editio minor* (for comparison between readings in HS_1 and HS_2 see vol. 3, xiii–xiv). Deviations from the text are noted in the commentary.

Each *Ennead* is referred to by Roman numerals, followed by the number of the treatise, the chapter of the treatise, and, finally, separated by a comma, the line number or numbers, for example, VI.8.8, 24–27, that is, *Ennead* VI, treatise number 8, Chapter 8, lines 24–27.

It is customary to add the chronological number given by Porphyry in his *Life of Plotinus* (*Vita Plotini*), so that, for example, VI.8 is designated VI.8 [39], that is, *Ennead* VI.8 is 39th in the chronological order. So we adopt the convention as follows: either VI.8.8, 1–5 (where the chronological number is not given) or VI.8 [39] 8, 1–5 (where it is given).

In this series the chronological number is given only in the Introduction and in other places where it may be of significance for understanding the chronological presentation of Plotinus' philosophical stance. The following chart indicates the chronological order.

Chronological Order of the *Enneads*

Enn.		*Enn.*		*Enn.*		*Enn.*		*Enn.*		*Enn.*	
I.1	**53**	II.1	**40**	III.1	**3**	IV.1	**21**	V.1	**10**	VI.1	**42**
I.2	**19**	II.2	**14**	III.2	**47**	IV.2	**4**	V.2	**11**	VI.2	**43**
I.3	**20**	II.3	**52**	III.3	**48**	IV.3	**27**	V.3	**49**	VI.3	**44**
I.4	**46**	II.4	**12**	III.4	**15**	IV.4	**28**	V.4	**7**	VI.4	**22**
I.5	**36**	II.5	**25**	III.5	**50**	IV.5	**29**	V.5	**32**	VI.5	**23**
I.6	**1**	II.6	**17**	III.6	**26**	IV.6	**41**	V.6	**24**	VI.6	**34**
I.7	**54**	II.7	**37**	III.7	**45**	IV.7	**2**	V.7	**18**	VI.7	**38**
I.8	**51**	II.8	**35**	III.8	**30**	IV.8	**6**	V.8	**31**	VI.8	**39**
I.9	**16**	II.9	**33**	III.9	**13**	IV.9	**8**	V.9	**5**	VI.9	**9**

	Enn.		*Enn.*		*Enn.*		*Enn.*		*Enn.*		*Enn.*
1	I.6	**10**	V.1	**19**	I.2	**28**	IV.4	**37**	II.7	**46**	I.4
2	IV.7	**11**	V.2	**20**	I.3	**29**	IV.5	**38**	VI.7	**47**	III.2
3	III.1	**12**	II.4	**21**	IV.1	**30**	III.8	**39**	VI.8	**48**	III.3
4	IV.2	**13**	III.9	**22**	VI.4	**31**	V.8	**40**	II.1	**49**	V.3
5	V.9	**14**	II.2	**23**	VI.5	**32**	V.5	**41**	IV.6	**50**	III.5
6	IV.8	**15**	III.4	**24**	V.6	**33**	II.9	**42**	VI.1	**51**	I.8
7	V.4	**16**	I.9	**25**	II.5	**34**	VI.6	**43**	VI.2	**52**	II.3
8	IV.9	**17**	II.6	**26**	III.6	**35**	II.8	**44**	VI.3	**53**	I.1
9	VI.9	**18**	V.7	**27**	IV.3	**36**	I.5	**45**	III.7	**54**	I.7

Synopsis

Chapter 1 — Well-being is a present disposition.

Chapter 2 — The actualized desire for life, well-being, is in the existent present.

Chapter 3 — The duration of time does not increase well-being.

Chapter 4 — More pleasure does not increase well-being.

Chapter 5 — Well-being over the course of life is the same as the well-being of the present.

Chapter 6 — Misery may increase over time but not well-being.

Chapter 7 — Well-being exists in the life of eternity not the unfolding of time.

Chapter 8 — Memory of the past does not increase the well-being of the present.

Chapter 9 — Memory of past beauty also does not affect the well-being of the present.

Chapter 10 — Well-Being is an inner disposition that causes virtue and fine actions.

Translation of Plotinus Ennead *1.5 [36]*

On Whether Well-Being Increases with Time

1. Does well-being increase with time, given that well-being is always regarded as [if it were] in the present moment? For memory of being happy does not produce well-being, nor [does] discussing it. Rather well-being exists somehow in a disposition.| Further, a disposition is in the present and the actuality of life.

2. But if because we always desire life and actuality, someone might suggest that obtaining well-being increases it more, first so that tomorrow's happiness will be greater and the next [day] always superior still | and well-being will no longer be measured by virtue. Even the gods will be happier now than before, but not yet perfectly so, never perfectly so. Then desire, attaining its end, has attained that which is present and always that which is present and

seeks to have well-being while it exists. So the desire | for life, as it seeks existence, is of the present, if existence is in the present. And even if the desire were for the future and what comes next, yet it wishes for what it has and is, not what is gone or what will come, but what already is, for this to exist, not seeking the forever, but for the already present to exist now.

3. What, then, about [the phrase] "He has been happier for more time and for more time he saw the same thing with his eyes"? Well, if he saw more accurately with more [time], then time would have produced something more for him. But if he saw to the same degree all along, | then, in seeing once, he has just as much [as the other].

4. But, [one might argue], the other man was pleased for a longer time.

But it would not be correct to count this toward well-being. And if someone were to characterize pleasure as unhindered activity, he is saying the same as what we are aiming at. And in any case | this greater pleasure only ever has what is present; its past pleasure has gone.

5. What then? If someone is happy from beginning to end [of his life] and another at a later time [of life] and [yet] another [was] first happy and then changed, is what they have equal? Here the comparison is not being made

between persons who are all happy, | but [the comparison is] between those who are not happy when they are not happy with those who are happy. So if one has more, he has as much as a happy person has in relation to the unhappy person, consequently his having more is in the present.

6. What then about the miserable? Does his misery not increase the longer he has it? And do not the rest of the vexations increase the misfortune with more time, such as long-lasting pain and grief and all things of this cast? | But if these things increase the evil with time, then why don't their opposites do the same for well-being?

One could say with respect to grief and pain that time brings about additional pain, as in the case of lingering illness; for a permanent condition arises and the body worsens more with time. | Since if the state remains the same and the damage is not made greater, then here too it is always the present that is painful, if one does not add the past in view of its having come to be and remaining; and with regard to the unhappy condition, the evil stretched out over more time increases the bad by persistence. | At any rate, one becomes miserable by the addition of a greater evil, not by an increase of the same [evil]. The more of the same does not exist simultaneously, and one ought not to speak in general of that as "more," reckoning what is no-longer with what is.

What concerns well-being, on the other hand, has a border and a limit and is always identical. But if someone says that here, too, there is an increase | with more time, that one is more happy the more one increases in virtue, his praise does not consist in reckoning the many years of his happiness, but when it is greater, then it is praised for being greater.

7. But why, if we ought only to consider the present and not to count it with the past, do we not do the same in the case of time, but, counting the past with the present, say that it is more? | Why then do we not say well-being is as much as the time that it lasts?

Then we would be dividing well-being according to the divisions of time; whereas, if we were measuring according to the present, we would make it indivisible. Now it is not unusual to count time even when it no longer exists, since we produce a count of things that have happened | and no longer are, like the dead; but it would be strange to say that well-being that no longer exists is more than what is present. For well-being requires continuance, while time needs to exist no longer than the present. Indeed, on the whole, more time | tends to the dispersal of a thing existing in the present. Due to this it is aptly called "image of eternity," as it tends to destroy the stability of eternity by its own dispersal. So that if it takes from eternity its quality of abiding in that realm and makes it its own, it destroys it—it being preserved for a time in a way by that [eternity], | while suffering destruction if it [eternity] should come to be altogether in it [sc. the temporal realm]. So if happiness is to be related to the good life, clearly then that life is to be reckoned as that of being, as this is the best. So then it should not be counted by time, but by eternity, for this is neither more nor less nor any length, but is a something, unextended | and not existent in time.

One must not, then, unite being with non-being, nor time nor the always of temporality with eternity, nor attribute extension to the unextended, but must grasp it all as a whole, if one is to grasp it at all, grasping not the undivided aspect of time, but the life of eternity, which is not composed of many times, | but from all of time all at once.

8. But if someone[42] says that memory of the past remaining in the present moment gives more to the one who has been happy a longer time, then what does he mean by memory? For if it is the memory of wisdom | previously having occurred, he will be saying that the person concerned *is* <now> wiser, and so would not be remaining true to the hypothesis. If it is the memory of pleasure, it will be

42 Likely Epicurus. See Diogenes Laertius, *Lives of the Eminent Philosophers* 10.11552.

as if the happy person needs an excess of enjoyment, not being content with what is present. And yet what pleasure does a memory of pleasure possess? For instance, if one were to remember | that yesterday one delighted in a fine dish? And ten years removed, that would be even more ridiculous. And so it is with wisdom, [the memory] that last year one was wise.

9. Well, if the memory were to be of fine things, would someone not be making a good point here? But this would pertain to a person who lacks fine things in the present and, not having them now, is seeking them in the memory of the past.

10. But [one might argue], length of time produces many fine actions, so that the person who is happy for a short period lacks his due portion—if indeed one should in general call happy one who is not so on the basis of the possession of many fine things.

Indeed, the one who says that well-being results from many | times and actions constructs well-being from items which no longer exist, but are in the past, and just one which is still present. It is for this reason that we postulated well-being as in the present, and then raised the question as to whether well-being is increased with more time. So we must inquire whether well-being over a long time | increases with more actions.

First of all, then, it is possible to become happy without actions, and to be not less but more so than the person of accomplishments. Then, actions do not confer well-being out of themselves, but one's dispositions are that which make actions fine. The wise person enjoys the fruits of the good even from his actions, not because | he acts, nor from the circumstances, but from out of that which he possesses. The saving of one's homeland can even come about through the agency of an individual of low moral standing, and so also the pleasure coming from the salvation of the homeland that a wise person enjoys, even though it came about through another. So this is not what produces the pleasure of happiness. Rather, it is one's disposition that produces | well-being and such pleasure as results from it. To place well-being in the sphere of actions is to situate it outside of virtue and the soul. For the activity of the soul resides in thought and being active within that sphere. It is in this that well-being consists.

Commentary

Chronologically, this is Plotinus' first attempt to offer his views on the practical implications for living the good life in conformity with his Platonic metaphysics and corresponding psychology. This text, as opposed to I.4 [46] *On Well-Being*, is more compact and less concerned with the overall life of the *eudaimōn* than with responding to those who argue that well-being is measured by duration (see Kalligas 2014, 188) or by a "complete life" (*Nichomachean Ethics* 1098a16–20). Written before his decline in health, this text reads less like a carefully planned theory and more like a hurried attempt to respond to one of the more attractive features of Stoicism and Epicureanism, that is, that human well-being is available to all in the present. Maintaining the attractiveness of an ethics that promises the immediacy of well-being regardless of one's circumstances, Plotinus is keen to establish the ontological grounds for his view of well-being in distinction from Aristotle and the Peripatetics as well as the Hellenistic schools. In this task, he both utilizes and adapts Stoic, Epicurean, and Aristotelian terminology into a Platonic framework. This is particularly clear in Plotinus' reformulation of well-being with a disposition (*diathesis*) situated in eternal as opposed to temporal life. Plotinus identifies living well with the life of eternity available to us via noetic contemplation so that the highest or "true" life of the human being, that it, its "natural inclination/desire" for which we are all actually oriented, is the unimpeded actualization of that part of ourselves which remains above or separate from our temporal, corporeal life. Overall, Plotinus synthesizes the Platonic concept of time as "the moving image of eternity" with his historical predecessors' views of the good life, virtue, and pleasure, in the hopes of offering a more robust vision of why a divine life is available to all in the immediacy of the present.

I will begin with a quick note on my seemingly inconsistent translation of the term *eudaimonia. Eudaimonia* has a long and arduous history of translation, often rendered as "happiness" or "flourishing" and connected to a kind of divine blessedness or, as Rist (1967, 140) reminds us, of "having one's daimon in good shape." I have decided on a kind of compromise, agreeing with, for the most part, Kalligas (2014, 162) and Armstrong (1984) in rendering *eudaimonia* as "well-being." The expression in the context of Plotinus, while sometimes clumsy, keeps readers cognizant of the metaphysical background of the height of human life, that is, that the *being* of being human, and by extension its good, is located in the life of the noetic which, *qua* absolute, lacks nothing, needs nothing, desires nothing. However, I have retained the use of "happiness" or "happy" at times, particularly when I believe Plotinus is referring to an interlocutor's naïve or incomplete conception of human well-being. The employment of both terms proves beneficial when Plotinus makes a distinction between a metaphysical conception of human well-being and the common notion of living a good life measured by duration, virtue and/or pleasure. Overall, contra Aristotle, well-being, for Plotinus, is in most instances not to be confused with the life well-lived, that is, the happy life defined by virtue, pleasure, or good luck. When I believe Plotinus is appealing to this distinction or making a nuance in light of this common misunderstanding, I have tried to make it clear in my translation by juxtaposing the two terms. Cf. Gerson (2018) who retains the use of "happiness" throughout his translation, due, I believe, to the need to address this common conception of *eudaimonia* present throughout the text. In any event, this is surely an instance where translation bleeds into interpretation.

Chapter 1

*The treatise opens with a stunning acceptance of a Stoic and Epicurean precept that human well-being belongs to the present moment and does not increase with more pleasure or with memory of past or anticipated joys. It succinctly rejects, however, the ontologies—or lack thereof—of Stoicism and Epicureanism; it also overrides a familiar Aristotelian concept that well-being results from virtuous action. Rather, Plotinus concludes this chapter by placing well-being in an inner disposition (*diathesis*) of the human soul, a disposition that moves human well-being from the world of becoming to the absolute activity of the intelligible.*

1, 1–2 *Does well-being increase . . . the present moment?*: The question whether well-being can be augmented over time, increasing or sustained with each day that one fares well and avoids exceeding misfortune (*Nicomachean Ethics* 1101a8–14 or 1100b28–30) or great tragedy, for example Priam's lamentable demise at the hands of the Achaeans (*Nicomachean Ethics* 1100a8–9), as the Aristotelian would claim, represents a category mistake for Plotinus. The mistake rests on a confusion regarding the nature of absolute well-being. True well-being is not available in the temporal world of process, where being never really *is* but always *becomes*. Those who would respond positively to the value of measuring well-being through a complete life (*Nicomachean Ethics*

1098a11 or 1099b10) err in not recognizing that well-being cannot be part of the sensible, corporeal world of becoming. Plotinus seems in agreement with the Epicurean and Stoic rejection of the need for temporal duration for human well-being. However, in this initial question, Plotinus lays the foundation for his very different ontological framework in his understanding of the present moment and its connection to the eternal world or that which is beyond temporality. By contrast, for the Epicurean, while past memories and anticipated joys may help one experience pleasure in the present, the experience is ultimately reserved for the present. This present is a simple site for the experience of pain or pleasure and it does not carry any more weight than an opportunity to remove either physical or psychic pain. For the Stoic, the present, in contradistinction to the past and future, is all that is "up to us," the past being fixed and the future always on the horizon. As such, we must concentrate our effort on understanding the freedom available to us right now in all that we think, say and do. This idea is seen in Marcus Aurelius' *Meditations*: "All those things, which you prayed to attain by a roundabout way, you can have right now, if you do not deny them to yourself. That is, if you leave the past and entrust the future to providence and direct the present to piety and justice" (12 1 1–2, trans. adapted from Haines). Again, like the Epicurean, this present moment, the right now, has no real ontological weight. For the Stoic, existence is not multi-layered but reserved to the material and corporeal. In contrast, for Plotinus, the present moment appeals to a thick layering of forms of life with absolute activity or intelligible life occupying the summit available to us right now. In short, the present moment is not merely a part of sequential chronological time, wherein what we experience is this moment as opposed to another. Rather, the present moment offers the opportunity to escape chronological time and elevate our form of life from that which is tied to sensible experience toward the transcendence available in the intelligible intellection of reality.

1, 2–3 *For memory of... not produce well-being*: This remark needs to be set in the context of Plotinus' overall account of memory where "memory, even if it is of the best things, is itself not one of the best things" (IV.4.4, 7–8). Markedly, Plotinus argues that there are two forms of memory: one of the higher soul in its residency with *Nous* and one of the lower, embodied soul. The former is associated with *recollecting* forms and realities while the lower is characterized as that which should be forgotten. See commentary below, especially Chapters 8 and 9. This latter form of memory occurs in time and is the result of the soul's descent into becoming—its wanton desire for individuality that must be shed if one is to ascend and return to the intelligible (IV.4.5, 24–30). Ultimately, for Plotinus there is a memory of what one is versus a memory that reduces the person to what one has: "For it could happen, even when one has no conscious awareness of having a memory, that one has it in oneself more strongly than if one knew that one did. For it could be that when one knows something, one might possess this as something different from oneself, while if one does not know that one has it, one may very well end up being what one has; and this latter experience actually makes the soul fall further" (IV.4.4, 12–15). Cf. IV.3.32, 13–19: "Indeed, to the extent that [the higher soul] strives upwards, it forgets more things—unless perhaps all its life even in the sensible world was somehow such that it has memories only of better things. In this connection, the remark about 'standing apart from human concerns' [*Phaedrus* 249c8–d1] is most apt; this necessarily comprises memory, too." Within the context of this passage on human well-being, it is clear that Plotinus refers to the latter of the two forms of memory, that is, corporeal, experiential memories, when emphasizing that memory does not participate in well-being. See Blumenthal (1971, 95–99), King (2009), and Warren (1965) for more on Plotinus' dual vision of memory as well as Gerson (1994, 180–183), who clarifies the loss of memory for an ascending soul: "This soul will not even remember that it engaged in philosophy and even that here it contemplated. It will remember neither intellectual nor sense-related activity. It is not possible, when engaged unqualifiedly in intellection, to remember anything (IV.4.1, 4–11). The ultimate destiny of the ideal self is as a subject eternally contemplating, bereft of memories altogether. It is united with Intellect substantially, although it has an awareness of itself being so united." Cf. IV.4.12, 49. For Plotinus' direct response to the Epicurean theory that memory of the past contributes to happiness see Commentary on Chapter 8.

1, 3–4 *Rather well-being exists . . . in a disposition*: As noted by Kalligas (2014, 188), Plotinus is directly challenging the Aristotelian concept of moral virtue as a *hexis* or "a disposition of the soul concerned with deliberate choice" (*Nicomachean Ethics* 1106b36–1107a1) as well as the Stoic conception that virtue is a bodily disposition (see Graeser, 1972, 24). Plotinus utilizes the idea that there is an inner disposition (*diathesis*) that is not consequent upon choice but is rather the underlying inclination of the soul. As a result of this position, Plotinus rejects the idea that one's disposition is simply the passive, material conditions or even the natural predilections of the soul-body composite or, more importantly, an accidental quality one possesses. Rather, this particular disposition (as there are others in the soul) is the authentic activity of the soul, its absolute life rooted in eternity. See Stamatellos (2015, 132) for Plotinus' distinction of *hexis* as a permanent state of the soul and *diathesis* as a more transient state. It seems that in this treatise, Plotinus is not using *diathesis* as a passive/temporary state but as a permanent inner disposition that intellectualizes the soul. On the permanence of disposition in all forms of life, see VI.1.11, 1–7. Cf. IV.3.12, 38; IV.3.13, 3; IV.3.24, 7; IV.4.45, 3;

IV.3.13, 5–18. Contra Stamatellos, this use of *diathesis* refers not to a transient quality in this passage. Rather, the appearance of transiency derives from the fact that there are varying dispositions in the embodied life of the human being that can be in tension with its intellectual life. For the soul's disposition to life, see III.4.5, 3. For its disposition to the universe, see III.4.6, 23. For the somatic or downward-leading disposition, see VI.3.16, 26 and IV.4.28, 29. For its dual disposition that can make the original disposition faint, see VI.7.5, 13–18. Cf. III.5.7, 45; IV.3.28, 18. For the universe's use of a varied sequence of dispositions so as to maintain the concordant dance of the heavens, see IV.4.33, 6 as well as IV.4.35, 45. On the universe receiving its varied dispositions from the demiurge, see VI.8.17, 9. On the possibility of mixed dispositions as a rejected explanation for evil, see I.8.12, 4. For another reference to this active disposition in the soul as that which constitutes the life of the true philosopher, that is, the one who experiences well-being, see V.9.2, 2. For how this inner/intellectual disposition is that which constitutes our divinity, see I.2.3, 19–23: "Indeed, as for such a disposition of the soul, one in which one thinks and is unaffected in this way, if someone were to say that it is a kind of assimilation to god, he would not be mistaken. For the divine is pure and this sort of activity, so that someone who imitates it has wisdom." On how this disposition transforms calculative reasoning in the intelligible world, see IV.3.18, 11–14: "If one takes calculative reasoning as that disposition which constantly derives from Intellect and is always present in souls, a stable activity and something like a reflection of it, then they would be using calculative reasoning even in the intelligible world." On how the intellectual soul remains undescended, existing transcendently above the sensible, corporeal world of becoming, see IV.8.8, 2–4: "[. . .] not even our own soul has descended entirely, but there is something of it always in the intelligible." Cf. IV.9.9, 7–22 where Plotinus clearly connects well-being and absolute intellectual life which reunites the human being with the divine: "For we are not cut off from [the divine] or separate, even if the nature of the body has intruded and drawn us to itself, but we breathe and are preserved because that Good has not given its gifts and then has gone away but is always bestowing them as long as it is what it is. But we exist more when we turn to him and our well-being is there, but being far from him is nothing else but existing less. There the soul takes its rest and is outside evils because it has run into the place which is clear of evils, and it thinks there, and is not passive, and its true life is there; for our present life, the life without God, is a trace of life imitating that life. But life in that realm is the active actuality of Intellect; and the active actuality generates gods in quiet contact with that Good, and generates beauty, and generates righteousness, and generates virtue. It is these the soul conceives when filled with God, and this is the beginning and end; its beginning because it comes from there, and its end because its good is there." See also I.2.3, 23–33 and V.3.4, 29–31.

1, 5 *Further a disposition . . . actuality of life*: Again, this disposition is the inner reality of the soul or, as we shall shortly see, the inner desire or inclination, which is always already sated due to its unity with the *Life* of Intellect. Put differently, since the soul already has/is eternal life and insofar as the present moment *is*, one's inner disposition will be the site of discovering or becoming aware of the intellect in us that is quietly contemplating reality in the eternal present. See III.7.11 for another reference to the eternal nature of this disposition. The language of actuality (*enérgeia*) in Chapter 1, 5 is, Aristotelian. Plotinus, however, transforms it to fit his metaphysical system; the sensory world is characterized by potency while the noetic is characterized by absolute actuality. While discussing the difference between potential and actual beings, Plotinus clarifies at II.5.3, 29–34: "For that which is potentially wants to be induced to actuality by the approach of something else in order that it might become something actually, but what itself possesses its eternal identity from itself, this would be actuality. All the first principles, then are actuality. For they possess what they should possess, from themselves and always." For Plotinus, the *actuality of life,* then, is the unhindered activity of eternal contemplation that constitutes all of intelligible reality. See also VI.7.17, 6–16.

Furthermore, this statement should also be read alongside I.4 where Plotinus distinguishes himself again from Aristotle, who failed to realize that life in its fullest sense belongs only to the transcendent, to that which lacks nothing and is therein not moving from potency to act but is simply act itself. See particularly I.4.3, 25–40: "If, then, living well belongs to something living fully—meaning to something that is in no way deficient in life—being happy will belong only to one living fully, for the best will belong to this, if indeed that which is really best in life, that is, the perfect life, is something that exists. For in this way, the goodness that exists in happiness would not be something superadded nor will something else from somewhere else provide the substrate for its being good. For what, added to a perfect life, would turn it into the best life? But if someone will say that what does this is the nature of the Good, that is a congenial argument to us, but now we are not seeking the cause of goodness, but that in which it exists. It has been said many times that the perfect life and the true and real life is in that intellectual nature and that the other sorts of life are imperfect and reflections of life and do not exist perfectly or purely and are no more lives than the opposite of this. And now let it be said summarily that so long as all living beings are from one source and they do not have life in the same way that it does, it is necessary that the source is the primary life, that is, the most perfect life." See also III.2.3, 36–41: "Some seem to share in existence alone, some in life, others more in the life of sense-perception while others again possess reason, and others have life in its entirety."

Chapter 2

The overall goal of Chapter 2 is best put into context with I 4.6, 17–18: *"The soul's desire is for that which is better than itself, by which, when it arrives, the soul is satisfied and at rest, and this is really the life that is willed." Here, the ultimate object of desire for the soul is the Good or One. For Plotinus, insofar as the soul has not fully descended, this Good is available to us in the absolutely existent present and, as such, we should not be distracted by desires arising from lack, desires which evidence the soul's imperfection and incompleteness. These are desires of the lower part of the soul, dragged down to the sensory, physical world of becoming and temporality. Rather, the desire for the Good is actualized desire or truly lived desire, complete and perfect in its satiation at the level of intellect. This is the highest end or* telos *of the soul, an activity of making the human soul like the divine, removing all otherness and obtaining that which we truly desire in keeping our will turned toward the Good/One.* Cf. VI.9.8, 34–45: *"That thing does not desire us, with the hope that it would be around us; rather, we desire it, and so are around it. And while we are always around it, we do not always look to it. We are like a chorus that, singing all the while, though relating to the chorus leader, may turn outwards from the spectacle, but when it does turn towards it, the chorus sings beautifully and does in truth relate to the chorus leader. So, too, we are always around it; when we aren't, then we will be completely dissolved, and will be no longer, but when we look towards it, that is 'journey's end and rest'* [Republic 532e], *and the end of discordance for us dancing round it a divinely inspired dance." In short, this chapter is ostensibly about the soul's true desire, a desire that does not arise from lack but from completeness, from* life itself, *a desire that is ultimately sated and therein cannot be augmented or increased.*

2, 1 *we always desire life and actuality*: Here the Greek is *ephesis*, but Plotinus also uses *erôs* and, more commonly, *orexis*, to express desire. See Gerson (1994, 151) for a discussion of this terminological obscurity amongst the Platonists. Desire in this context is also connected to Plotinus' use of *boulêsis* as a kind of intellectual desire for the good wherein the will is a willing for itself, for its own perfection or actuality. See VI.8.6, 34–42 and IV.4.12, 44–46. Primarily, Plotinus is drawing on and adapting the Socratic/Platonic doctrine that all human beings desire or will the good, that is, that no one ever willingly aims at the bad or desires the bad. Expanding this psychological claim about human desire to include an ontological basis for all action and deliberation, Plotinus emphasizes that the soul desires absolute and actual life versus seeming or imperfect life. This, of course, draws on the already noted Aristotelian conception of actuality and the ontological priority of act over potency whereby act is the cause of movement, bringing what is merely potential or drawing potential being to its end. Again, see II.5 (quoted in part above) for Plotinus' discussion of potential versus actual being. In short, what the human soul desires is to be free from potency, or that which is tied to matter, and to be identified with eternal substance. For Plotinus, activity toward the lower sphere, that is, misdirected desire, resembles the higher or truer desire insofar as even in our confusion we do not will potential but actual being. Stated bluntly, we never will the bad as the will is always directed toward the good. Again, see above I.4.17; VI.9.8, and IV.9.9, 7–22, where Plotinus describes the true desire of the soul as fully actualized life, that is, the soul that has turned to intelligible contemplation of the Good. Plotinus is contrasting this always sated desire, meaning the actuality or life of the soul in contemplation of the Good, with a more commonplace conception of desire as that which is excessive or insatiable, namely, the kinds of desire met by sensible objects or the variations of desire that are never truly sated but are simply compounded and infinitely excessive. This juxtaposition is at the heart of the confusion of those who think that human well-being can be increased from one moment to the next. There is here a failure to understand that well-being is the inner disposition of the soul in its reversion to and contemplation of itself and its causes. Unless one turns within and discovers the always already sated desire of the soul constituting its eternal life, its intellectual disposition, one shall only be half-heartedly mollified by that which, in its nature, cannot satisfy the soul. On the intellectual desire of the soul and its turning either inward to what sates it or outward to the world in which it will eventually forget itself, see IV.8.4 and II.3.9, 24–27. On the connection of disposition to desire and how that desire can be misdirected in the sensible world, see particularly II.3.11, 3–15: "For example, if it is fire, the fire here is dim in comparison, and if it is a disposition (*diathesis*) to friendship, it becomes weak in the one who received it and the friendship it produces is not particularly beautiful, and indeed, spiritedness, not being received in due measure so that one becomes courageous, produces either rage or faintheartedness, and the disposition of being in love with honor and concerned with its beauty produces a desire for things that appear beautiful, and what flows out from intellect produces clever trickery. For even clever trickery wants to be intellect, but it is not able to achieve what it desires. Each of these dispositions, then, comes to be bad in us, although they were not bad in the heavenly region. For not only are they not what they were there, they do not even remain such as they were when they arrived, since they become mixed with bodies and matter and one another."

2, 5 *measured by virtue*: By thinking of well-being as something that can be increased by duration, Plotinus criticizes Aristotle and the Peripatetics. Namely, he takes them to task for a contradiction implicit in their ethical system: that if happiness is measured by a complete life so that each instance of happiness needs to be added up over the course of one's life, then happiness is measured not by virtue but by duration. To be sure, Plotinus is being polemical here, as he simply does not subscribe to the Aristotelian idea that well-being is measured by virtue, if by virtue one means moral/practical virtue. For Plotinus, such virtue is a consequence of well-being rather than the activity that constitutes well-being. For Plotinus, virtue is understood on a five-fold schema (see I.2), beginning with 1) a lower form of civic virtue before turning to the higher virtues of 2) purifying, 3) contemplative, 4) intellectual, and 5) exemplary. The first level, civic virtue, was considered by Plotinus to be outside the purview of the divine life. Plotinus was more interested in the higher forms of virtue as they focused on assisting practitioners to heed the Platonic/Socratic dictum of the *Theaetetus* (176d1–2): "assimilation to God." Ultimately, this was less of an ethic than a prescription for discovering the true nature of the human being and the human being's well-being at the level of the intellect. See particularly I.2.3, 1–10. Cf. *Theaetetus* 176b1, *Republic* 430c and *Phaedo* 69b–c. Overall, virtue, for Plotinus, is not a practical activity leading to the good life. Rather, it is a purification that allows one to recover/discover one's transcendent state—the fact that one is already separate and divine—via tapping into the highest part of the soul absolutely freed from the body and its trappings. See I.2.6, 14–24, where Plotinus describes the transcendent "virtue" of a person who has achieved this state. Overall, virtue is not technically part of the well-being of the soul at the level of intellect, if by virtue one means behaving justly, piously, and prudently in this world. However, if virtue is understood as the activity of separating oneself from the body and becoming like a God, Plotinus would then approve of virtue as a measure for human well-being, as it would correspond to the activity of coming to identify oneself with the level of intellect. Again, though, if one means moral or civic virtue, then Plotinus' statement in this passage is purely an attempt to undermine his interlocutor by using their own premises. See also I.2.4, 18, where Plotinus identifies the soul's virtue with its purification, which he describes as a "turning of the soul" (*epistrophe*). On the above desire of the soul and its relationship to purification, see particularly I.6.7, 1–12: "We must, then, ascend to the Good, which every soul desires. If someone, then, has seen it, he knows what I mean when I say how beautiful it is. For it is desired as good, and the desire is directed to it as this, though the attainment of it is for those who ascend upward and revert to it and who divest themselves of the garments they put on when they descended. It is just like those who ascend to partake of the sacred religious rites where there are acts of purification and the stripping off of the cloaks they had worn before they go inside naked. One proceeds in the ascent, passing by all that is alien to the god until one sees by oneself alone that which is itself alone uncorrupted, simple, and pure, that upon which everything depends, and in relation to which one looks and exists and lives and thinks."

2, 5–6 *Even the gods . . . never perfectly so*: As Kalligas notes (2014, 189), this aside is directed at Aristotle, consisting in a direct attack against his argument that the gods possess perfect and complete happiness. Cf. *Nicomachean Ethics* 1178b7–9. Moreover, this could also be directed at the Epicureans who held similar ideals about the divine regardless of its corporeality. Cf. Epicurus, *Letter to Menoeceus* 123–124. See also I.4.4, 1–5, where Plotinus emphasizes the perfection and well-being of the divine and his parallel belief that this perfect life belongs to the human being as well.

2, 7–9 *Then desire, attaining . . . while it exists*: Kalligas (2014, 189) translates desire here as "propensity" and cites the *Symposium* 200d3–6 to draw out a parallel to Diotima's speech that human desire is for our present life and not for the past or the future. While the parallel is apt, as Plotinus will shortly dismiss the value of the past and future, the concord between Diotima's speech and this passage consists in the notion that true desire, or desire understood correctly, will be for that which one has, the inner disposition focused on the contemplation of reality and the Good from which it has sprung, and for that to exist always, that is, eternally. Here, Plotinus is more concerned with demarcating existence or reality as that which is both 1) present and 2) *existing* in the present than juxtaposing forms of life (albeit this is an implicit implication). Put otherwise, the focus in this passage is on the coincidence of the present and absolute existence—a coincidence that substantiates the satiation of our desire, that is, that desire has reached its limit or end in the absolutely existent present. Thus, Plotinus is beginning to situate the good life in the realm of *Nous* and the *Life* of eternity. Cf. III.7.3, 15–23 as well as III.7.5, 25–30, where Plotinus tacitly agrees with Aristotle that the good life is in the complete life, but only if one is not measuring the complete life in time but in the absolute wholeness of eternity existent in the present: "And if one were to call eternity in this way life, that is, unlimited from the start because it is whole and does not expend anything of itself due to the fact that it has no past and no future—for if it did, it would not be whole—one would be getting close to a definition." Cf. Seneca, *Letter to Lucilius* 78.14.

2, 9–13 *So the desire . . . to exist now.* It is interesting, first and foremost, to note Plotinus' shift in vocabulary from desire *(ephesis)* to wish *(thelein)* over the more metaphysically loaded term for willing (*boulêsis*). Plass (1982) and McGroaty (2006, 111) argue that *thelein*, unlike willing (*boulêsis)*, is an expression of wishing for material necessities or externals, while *boulêsis* is the willing for the good. This distinction though seems to be problematized here, as Plotinus argues that the "wish" is actually directed at the absolute. It is possible that this is an instance wherein *thelein* expresses the soul's desire for that which *is* versus that which *becomes*, or, perhaps, this is simply a terminological inconsistency.

Nevertheless, it could be that Plotinus intentionally switches vocabulary, to exhibit how one who "wishes" for the future—something not yet and never—actually desires or wants what one already has, something ever present and eternal. This would be a nice way for Plotinus to show that "no one willingly errs" insofar as all our wishes, even for the bad, are simply perversions of what we all truly desire, Being and the Good. Cf. *Gorgias* 466a8–468e5. Furthermore, in this passage, Plotinus is, for the first time, suggesting that the future *qua* future does exist in full propriety insofar as only the present can properly be said to be. As such, when one desires or wishes for the future, and when that desire is for something existent, then one is simply desiring the being and reality of the now. Kalligas (2014, 189) suggests the deletion of the second *êdê*, as he believes it "attaches an unwarranted temporality to the final 'to exist.'" However, in the context of this discussion, the *êdê* serves as a reinforcement of the value of the present moment, that is, the now or the present is what we truly desire versus a seeking of forever. In short, the *êdê* reinforces once again that only in the "now" and not in the past or future will well-being be discovered as only the "now" escapes temporality or chronological/sequential time. Forever, or that which lasts for an infinite amount of time, pales in comparison with the singularity and completeness of the present. In short, there is repose/completion in the now as opposed to the interminable, insatiable seeking of the forever. Rist (1967, 148) argues that due to the combination of a) the fact that there is a part of the human soul that always remains in Intellect, fully identical with eternal life and hence always available in the present, and b) that the sage is happy even when he is unconscious, for example sleeping, the conclusion follows that, for Plotinus, "everyone is happy all the time." McGroarty (2014, 87 and 147n23) contends against this thesis, arguing that this view of Rist "is clearly false" or "is demonstrably false," citing I.5.2, 4–5 as supporting, incorrectly, the view that Plotinus believes that *eudaimonia* is measured by virtue as well as the more convincing III.2.4, 45–47, which emphasizes that only the good are happy, or III.2.5, which suggests that the inability to be happy is due to human weakness. There is merit to both Rist and McGroarty's claims insofar as well-being is part and parcel of the inner disposition constituting the true life of the soul, whether one is aware of it or not. Rist's view follows the later Neoplatonists like Proclus who lambasted Plotinus' view on well-being for just this reason. Cf. Proclus, *Commentary on Plato's Timaeus* III 334.10–14: "If the best part of our being is perfect, then the whole of our being must be well-off. But in that case, why are we humans at this very moment not all of us well-off, if the summit of ourselves indulges in perpetual intellection and is constantly in the presence of gods." Nevertheless, McGroarty is also correct to insist that for Plotinus we are required actively to turn toward this higher part of ourselves, to be disposed to this higher part, so as to become unified with it. Otherwise, we are merely resting easy with the faint impression of our well-being versus becoming identical to it. Cf. I.2.4, 20–30: "Did it, therefore, neither have them nor recollect them? In fact, it had things that were not active, but dispersed and un-illuminated. If they are to be illuminated and it is to know them as being present, it must impel itself towards that which does the illuminating. And it did not have the things themselves, but the impressions. It must, then, harmonize the impressions with the true Beings of which they are impressions. And perhaps it is in this sense that this nature 'has' them, because the Intellect is not alien to it, especially not when it looks toward the Intellect. If this were not so, the Intellect would be alien even when it is present. For even areas of scientific understanding in which we are not wholly engaged are alien."

Chapter 3, 4 and 5

Totaling fifteen succinct lines, these three chapters are significant insofar as they undergird Plotinus' adaptation of both Aristotelian and Epicurean theories of pleasure. In this adaptation, Plotinus, while rejecting the role of pleasure in the life of well-being, wields both theories to outline the nature and perfection of the good available in the present. See Van Riel *(2000) for the definitive treatment of pleasure in Plato, Aristotle, and the Neoplatonists. Van Riel outlines Plato's conception of pleasure as deriving from a replenishment/return to a natural condition or a necessary excess that "always admits of the more or less" (*Philebus *27e5–28a4). He further highlights Aristotle's rejection of Plato's account insofar as pleasure for Aristotle is that which follows from an unimpeded activity of a disposition in its natural state (*Nicomachean Ethics *1153a 12–15). Pleasure is that which perfects natural activities, be they bodily or psychic (Nicomachean Ethics 1174b 31–33). As Van Riel (2000, 52) succinctly states, "Pleasure is not the return to the natural condition; on the contrary, it is the perfect realization of the activity that is inherent in the natural condition itself." For Aristotle, human well-being, insofar as it is measured by a particularly human virtue, that is, the exercise of the rational faculty, will necessarily be accompanied with pleasure when it does its proper work or function so that the intellectual life will be a pleasurable life. Furthermore, for Aristotle all pleasure is complete insofar* *as it is pleasure, but intellectual activity leads to a form of pleasure that is stable and at rest. For Aristotle's account of pleasure at rest, see* Nicomachean Ethics *1154b26–28 where he writes on the "pleasure" of the divine in its act of thinking: "Hence god enjoys a simple single pleasure perpetually. For there is not only an activity of motion, but also an activity of immobility, and pleasure exists rather in rest than in motion." Cf.* Nicomachean Ethics *1177a25–27: "At all events the pursuit of it [philosophic wisdom] is thought to offer pleasures marvelous for their purity and their enduringness" (trans. Ross). This conception of pleasure foreshadows the Epicurean distinction between kinetic and katastematic pleasure, with the latter form being defined as the complete absence of pain, that is, a form of pleasure that does not derive from movement, for example eating or drinking. Katastematic pleasures are the basis for human well-being because kinetic pleasures are always connected to the continued, unlimited removal of pain while katastematic pleasures have a natural limit. See Cicero,* De finibus *II 9; Diogenes Laertius,* Lives of the Eminent Philosophers *X 136; Van Riel (2000, 85) for his concise explanation of Epicurean prudence in relation to discovering the limit of pleasure.*

Finally, Plotinus synthesizes the various views of his predecessors while insisting that pain and pleasure are not experiences of the soul but of the body; the soul merely understands or recognizes that the body is undergoing the affection. See IV.4.18,

9–10. Overall, since Plotinus returns to the more Platonic conception of pleasure as a restoration or satiation of a need, then what follows is the idea that the more the human being identifies with that which is already sated, that is, with the undescended soul residing at the level of intellect, the less such a person would experience pleasure. See VI.7.29, 7–10 and I.4.2, 1–25. Consequently, for Plotinus pleasure, as it is customarily understood, is not part of well-being. Nevertheless, Plotinus does seem to admit of a qualifiedly different form of pleasure for the one who has achieved well-being. See I.4.12, 1–12: "The virtuous person is always content and his state is one of tranquility, his disposition is lovable, and no one of the things said to be evil disturbs him, if he is virtuous. If, though, someone seeks to discover some other form of pleasure in the virtuous life, he is not seeking the virtuous life." As Van Riel (2000, 116) observes, this passage brings Plotinus close to the image of the Epicurean sage, except that the life of such a sage is based in an immaterial form of being in the world. There also seems to be a kind of joy or qualitatively different form of pleasure in those who have ascended to the highest levels of intellection, taking in the vision of the Good. See I.6.7, 12–15: "And, then, if someone sees this, what pangs of love will he feel, what longing and, wanting to be united with it, how would he not be overcome with pleasure?" Overall, the following section in I.5 will describe the life of well-being in the same terms and conditions as the life of pleasure in both Aristotle and Epicurus; that well-being is the unimpeded activity of a natural disposition that is measured by a limit. In other words, despite not being an account of pleasure, but of the radically other ontological reality where pleasure either does not exist or is of a radically other manifestation, well-being is still described by Plotinus in terms of limit and unimpeded activity, indicating a decisively Aristotelian and Epicurean heritage.

3, 1–5 *What, then, about . . . just as much [as the other]*: Also noted by Kalligas (2014, 189), consider *Nicomachean Ethics* 1174a14–19, where Aristotle compares the completeness of sight to pleasure: "Now the act of sight appears to be perfect at any moment of its duration; it does not require anything to supervene later in order to perfect its specific quality. But pleasure also appears to be a thing of this nature. For it is a whole, and one cannot at any moment put one's hand on a pleasure which will only exhibit its specific quality perfectly if its duration be prolonged" (trans. Rackham). Here, Plotinus is beginning to lay out his fundamental agreement both with Aristotle and with Epicurus that the highest good be complete in the activity. In other words, despite the fact that both Aristotle and, consequently, Epicurus will use this example to emphasize the complete activity that constitutes pleasure (as opposed to a movement in time which is never fully realized in the present moment), Plotinus uses this long-standing example to shift from the completion of pleasure in the present moment to the metaphysical ascent possible in the present moment. That is, well-being for Plotinus is comparable to Aristotle's and Epicurus' conception of pleasure as an activity (*energeia*) at rest or without movement. Under Plotinus' account this activity is reformulated in order to emphasize that the only complete activity for the soul is the life of intellect, a life free from affection and, accordingly, pleasure.

4, 1–4 *But, [one might argue] . . . the other . . . are aiming at*: This sentence is directed against the Aristotelian concept of pleasure, which is defined as what follows from an unhindered activity resulting from a natural disposition. At the same time, Plotinus shows a strong agreement with the Epicurean idea that infinite and finite experience of the good are equal. As such, Plotinus offers a unique synthesis. For *tên energeian tên anempodiston*, see Aristotle *Nicomachean Ethics* 1153a12–16: "For pleasures are not really processes, nor are they all incidental to a process: they are activities, and therefore an end; nor do they result from the process of acquiring our faculties, but from their exercise; nor have they all of them some end other than themselves: this is only true of the pleasures of progress towards the perfection of our nature. Hence it is not correct to define pleasure as a conscious process; the term should rather be 'activity of our natural state,' and for 'conscious' we must substitute 'unimpeded.'"

4, 4–5 *And in any case this greater pleasure only ever has what is present; its past pleasure has gone*: The greater pleasure for Plotinus resembles the Aristotelian and Epicurean concept of pure pleasure or complete pleasure insofar as, like the Aristotelian and Epicurean notions, this pleasure is not increased or decreased but is complete in itself. Nevertheless, insofar as Plotinus distinguishes corporeal from intelligible "pleasure" (this pleasure is not an affection), this greater pleasure at the level of the intellect is outside of time and separate from the processes of the body-soul composite. This escape from temporal movement is crucial to Plotinus' arguments regarding the completeness of this "greater pleasure," suggesting that the Epicurean dependency on experience and sensibility make "complete pleasure" or katastematic pleasure impossible. Nothing of the material, corporeal world can truly be sated but is always only in transit. The Aristotelian pleasure, too, follows from the actualization of a natural disposition; as such, in Plotinus it has been transplanted to an ontological playing field outside embodiment into the realm of the separable intellectual soul, that is, into our true disposition or nature.

5, 1–7 *What then? If . . . in the present*: Cf. Aristotle, *Nicomachean Ethics* 1100a33–1100b7. Here Plotinus offers us three different portraits of well-being, all of which do not square with his own conception of well-being. First, there is the person who has lived a complete life. Second, the person who becomes happy later in life and, finally, the person, like Priam, who was happy but suffered great misfortune and seemingly loses his happiness. In asking if their happiness or well-being is equal, Plotinus is mitigating a concern, namely that the person who has well-being in the present moment is equal to the person who possesses it for a longer duration. This strikes most people as patently false. Yet, Plotinus cleverly attempts to show that by comparing all three, you are comparing them all when they are not actually doing well, that is, you are comparing souls at the level of embodiment. In other words, you are comparing them all when they are not happy or doing well. None of these lives represent authentic well-being but are simply instances of the good life lived in time. The last line, "*if one has more*," reorients the reader to the locus of the ontological "more" of human well-being that exists in the present. This present well-being is absolute as opposed to the instances of happiness that do not constitute such transcendent well-being. So if one actually has "more" well-being, this is a matter of actually doing well by transcending the body and achieving authentic human well-being or the well-being of the sage in comparison to those who may be living a virtuous and good life but are not at the level of authentic well-being.

Chapter 6

This section of the treatise has, in some senses, the feel of a "bait and switch" maneuver. Beginning with a discussion of misery and pain, readers are asked to consider first how the common conception of pain fails to compare to human well-being, particularly when it comes to the question of whether either pain or well-being can be increased with more time. Unlike well-being, pain, and misery seem to be things which can be increased, because discomfort and suffering are attributes of the body-soul composite and, as such, are subject to time/duration. Moreover, torment that persists can permanently cripple the body-soul composite, therein hindering intellectual activity. As interesting as this disanalogy between well-being and pain may be, the goal in this chapter revolves around how pain only exists in the present moment. In this way, Plotinus emphasizes that existence is always in the present and that this existence is always absolutely what it is, needing no duration or addition. This thesis is prepared for by accentuating how if the pain of the present is increased, it is because new "evil" or a different or more intense pain has been added to it. Plotinus asks us to keep in mind that each instance of the same pain, regardless of duration, is equal. Since we only experience the present we are not actually increasing our experience of pain or misery unless a qualitatively new pain or misery is introduced. Here, we see how Plotinus' quick excursus on pain is a sleight of hand, as understanding the nature of pain is not his objective. Rather, he is more concerned with showing how the present moment is the residence of that which is limited or self-identical and therein qualitatively different than the parts of time, namely, past and future or that which does not fully partake in reality but is an always-has-been or an always-will-be. In the present moment pain and pleasure are equal but, more importantly, well-being in its fullness can be achieved because, unlike the past or future, the present moment is. The reality of the present moment gives the individual the opportunity to recognize not only Being but the Life of eternity. This recognition allows one to identify not with the pain or pleasure of the embodied soul, but that which is separate from the materiality of things, that which is absolutely so that the present moment acts as a permanently open invitation for transcendence. Furthermore, insofar as human well-being has a limit or is absolute, Plotinus is also keen to show how unlike the pursuit of virtue, particularly civic virtue, well-being is not a process originating from lack or a striving or a process of increasing virtue. For an Aristotelian this would seem strange, as the life of ever-increasing virtue constitutes human flourishing. However, for Plotinus virtue and human well-being are not identical, particularly if virtue is located in the goings-on of the body/soul composite. When one praises someone for becoming increasingly more virtuous, one praises activities in time, praising the expansion rather than simplicity of being. In short, the entire discussion of the nature of pain leads to a reiteration that there is a limit to human well-being, a limit drawn by the perfection of intelligible reality available in the existent present.

6, 1–6 *What then about . . . for well-being*: Attempting to lull his reader into a sense of familiarity with regard to common conceptions of human well-being, Plotinus shows a great deal of sympathy for his interlocutor, recognizing that an allowance seems warranted in the case of prolonged pain. One is obviously worse off the longer one is worse off and, as such, well-being, as the seeming opposite of human misery, must also be subject to increase. It is to be expected that Plotinus uses pain and grief as examples of human misery, given that both reflect the soul that has become attached to the life of the body-soul composite. See IV.4.19, 1–5. In I.5, Plotinus undermines the common notion that pain can be increased in two ways. The first is by way of concession, as he grants that pain, if experienced for a long time, can bring about a permanent condition; moreover, this condition makes it impossible to turn to the higher part of the soul. He says as much at I.8.8, 34–35 while discussing how a bad bodily constitution can restrict the powers of judgment, making those who fret about the body unstable, indulging in the pain their body is experiencing versus recognizing it as something which is theirs or, at least, a part of that which is theirs, their body, versus that which is really themselves, their soul. In this sense, bodily pain can tempt the soul into forgetting itself, thereby regressing, as it were, into a permanent bodily condition. It also chains the soul to a corporeal life, an unnatural and therein painful disposition (*hexis*) for the human being, whose being belongs not to the corporeal but to the intelligible. This, I believe, is the truer evil for Plotinus, that is, not pain or grief as such, insofar as the healthy soul or the soul that recognizes its transcendent state will simply observe and recognize the pain and misery of the embodied soul but will not be subsumed by it. In contradistinction, the soul that has turned its gaze outward, and continuously or predominantly so falls into a condition wherein it identifies with the pain and grief, rendering it unable to see itself as what it is, rendering it unable to see itself as anything other than pain and grief. However, this concession to the reality of long-lasting pain actually increasing via time is immediately destabilized in the following section.

6, 6–18 *One could say . . . with what is*: Here, Plotinus is both leaning on the Epicurean adages that venerate the present moment as the site of all experience as well as on the belief that long-lasting pain is tolerable. Agreeing with the Epicurean belief on the basis that all that we experience is the present, Plotinus also adds the addendum that long lasting pain is tolerable not simply because it does not kill an individual but also because the present is the site of absolute existence. Most focus on adding the present with the past, but for Plotinus that would be adding what does not exist, or does not fully exist, to what exists in full, a state that needs no more than what it has. Furthermore, if pain is persistent, then you are experiencing not more but the same, because, again, the present is all that is experienced. Even if you experience a qualitatively different pain from one moment to the next, you simply experience a different pain and not more, as the preceding pain is gone and done and, therein, cannot be measured with the current pain.

6, 18–23 *What concerns well-being . . . has a border and a limit . . . for being greater*: By appealing to the limit of well-being Plotinus puts himself squarely in conversation with his Epicurean counterparts who would have aligned katastematic pleasure, or the highest form of pleasure, with the limited. Cf. Cicero *de finibus* 1.11.37: "A man who is conscious of his condition at all must necessarily feel either pleasure or pain. But complete absence of pain Epicurus considers to be the limit and highest point of pleasure; beyond this point pleasure may vary in kind, but it cannot vary in intensity or degree." As we have observed, this Epicurean position is famously foreshadowed in Aristotle, who argued for a difference between natural pleasures and incidental pleasures. As Van Riel (2000, 81) highlighted, this is contrary to Plato's *Philebus*, wherein pleasure is associated with unlimited need and the constant seeking of replenishment. Contrariwise for Aristotle, natural pleasures are supervenient on a fulfillment of one's disposition while incidental pleasures result from a process or from a movement that has no natural end. This, then, foreshadows the Epicurean concepts of kinetic and katastematic pleasure. See *Nicomachean Ethics* 1154b15–20: "But the pleasures that do not involve pains do not admit of excess; and these are among the things pleasant by nature and not incidentally. By things pleasant incidentally I mean those that act as cures (for because as a result people are cured, through some action of the part that remains healthy, for this reason the process is thought pleasant); by things naturally pleasant I mean those that stimulate the action of the healthy nature" (trans. Ross).

Chapter 7

Certainly the densest in the treatise, this chapter is best read alongside III.7 On Eternity and Time. *In Chapter 7 Plotinus will appeal to his own unique conception of time and eternity, emphasizing for readers why well-being cannot be measured by duration, as it is qualitatively different than the temporal life. In III.7 Plotinus is eager to discuss the life of soul and its relation to time as well as the fact that the highest disposition of soul remains at the level of intellect and therein lives in eternity. Repeatedly, Plotinus invokes the idea that despite being creatures of time, that is, despite the fact that we are the product of the procession from and departure out of Being and the life of eternity, we still have contact with eternity. As he rhetorically questions, "For what comprehension could we have of eternity if we were not in direct contact with it? How could we be in contact with what is alien? We, too, then, must participate in eternity" (III.7.7, 3–5). This share in eternity is our true life, the life we would live if we did not wander outward toward the life of making and production, of extension and interval, of difference and repetition. As he asks, "What, then, do we say of someone who does not put aside his contemplation of such an object, but stays with it in awe of its nature and is able to do this with his own indefatigable nature? In fact, he will be a man racing into eternity and not faltering in his effort to be made the same as it and to be eternal by contemplating eternity and the eternal with the eternal in himself" (III.7.5, 8–13). Here, Plotinus is already envisioning the soul's well-being as situated in intellectual contemplation transcendently other than the Aristotelian or Stoic contemplative life. Interestingly though, this well-being is consistently set in contrast to the soul's original outgoing, highlighting, therein, the difficulty of the soul's return. See III.7.11, 19–34: "For since there was in soul a power that was not quiet and wanted to keep changing into something else what it saw in the intelligible world, it was not willing to have everything present to it all together. But just as the expressed principle unfurls itself from a dormant seed and makes a transition, as it thinks, to something large, obliterating the largeness by the fact that it has divided itself, and instead of a unity in itself, it squanders its unity no longer in itself and proceeds to a weaker extension; indeed, in the same way, the soul, too, as it produces, in imitation of the intelligible world, a sensible world which moves not with the motion found in the intelligible world, but one that aims to have the sameness of an image, temporalized itself by creating time in place of eternity." Later Plotinus clarifies how time and eternity represent two fundamentally and qualitatively different forms of Life. He emphasizes that time is the "spreading out of life" in perpetual and everlasting continuity so that past and future are parts of time, partaking in a kind of existence that images reality. Cf. III.7.11, 42–58: "The extension of life, then, involves time, the ceaseless progression of life involves the ceaseless time and life which has passed involves past time. Would it then make any sense to say that time is the life of the soul in its changing motion from one way of living to another? For if eternity is life in stability, identity, and sameness, and is unlimited from the start, and time must be an image of eternity, just as this universe is related to the one above, then instead of the life above we must say equivocally, in a way, that there is another life, that of this power of the soul. And instead of identity, sameness, and remaining in itself, there is not remaining in itself but exercising different actions, instead of the unextended and unity, the image of unity, the unity found in continuity; instead of being unlimited from the start and whole, there is the progression to infinity leading to continuous succession, and instead of the whole being gathered together, the whole which will and will forever be is going to exist, part by part. For in this way, it will imitate what is whole from the start, together and unlimited from the beginning, if it wants to be always gaining something in its existence. For in this way, its existence will imitate that of the intelligible world." See also III.7.5, 9–13 and III.7.12.*

7, 1–3 *But why, if . . . it is more?*: Plotinus' aim is to separate his view from philosophies that emptied time of reality, for example the Stoic and the Epicurean philosophies as well as Aristotle's, who regarded the motion of bodies to have ontological priority over time. Kalligas notes that for the Stoic, "only the present exists" while the past and future subsist (*huphestōs*) (2014, 188 and 190, cf. *SVF* II 509 and 518).

This distinction between subsisting versus actual existence alludes to the strange liminal space of the "incorporeals" in Stoic philosophy. Insofar as there was a strict dichotomy between being and not-being, the bodiless reality of time was a problem and as such—alongside space and sayings or expressions, in addition to the void—time was described as a kind of "something," that is, that which is not wholly real but having some part to play in reality. See also III.7.8 for Plotinus' critique of the Stoic conception of time as the extension of bodies in motion. For confirmation of this view, see *SVF*, I 26, 11–15, II 164, 14, II 166, 8–10, II 509, II 510 as well as II 521. Overall, the Stoics, for the most part, regarded time as a kind of continuum, infinitely divisible and extended in all directions, with past and future being the parts of time that *subsist* while the present *belongs* (Stobaeus I 106, 19–23 = *SVF* 2 509). One of the paradoxes that arose from this view is the "measure" of the present moment and its concomitant ambiguous reality. See Plutarch, *On Common Conceptions* 1081c–1082a. See Marcus Aurelius, *Meditations* III.10 and 12 as well as IV.43, IV.48, and IV.42 for the moral implications of the Stoic valorization of the present moment, which parallels Plotinus' views on the value of the present in this treatise. This emptying of the ontological reality of time takes a further turn in the Epicurean who is reported to have seen time as a *phantasma*. See Sextus Empiricus, *Against the Mathematicians* X. 181 as well as Epicurus, *Letter to Herodotus* 72–73 (quoted in full in the Introduction to the

Treatise). In contradistinction to both these schools, time and all its parts are a kind of reality for Plotinus. Unlike the Stoic, Plotinus valorizes, versus dismisses, the incorporeal nature of time, elevating it above body and the movement of bodies. Overall, for Plotinus, time is not a lower form of reality but an epiphenomenon or product of reality. While it is true that only the present moment exists in full propriety, the past and future are also existent as parts of time, that is, as shares of the unfolding of being in becoming. Consider III.7.13, 50–54: "But if someone were to say that time is not existent, it is clear that he would have to state that he was making a false statement, whenever he says 'was' and 'will be.' For 'will be' and 'was' have the same existence as that in which he says he 'will be.'" Finally, while rejecting Aristotle's conception of time as derivative of movement, as its measure, Plotinus is appealing to the Aristotelian argument that "time is the number of motion with respect to before and after, and is continuous because it is an attribute of something continuous." While he does not agree with this, he utilizes the idea that time is a kind of counting up so as to transplant this counting up of time to the question of whether well-being should be counted and subject to this count as well. As we shall see, he utilizes this theory but ultimately rejects that either well-being or time can be reduced to a count or measure. Rather, they are forms of life.

7, 5–6 *Why then do . . . divisions of time*: Here, whether Plotinus is referring to abstract divisions of time like past, present, and future or to concrete measures like hour, day, or month is unclear. If to the latter then Plotinus may be gesturing to his own refutation of Aristotle's theory of time as a measure and number. See Aristotle, *Physics* IV 11 218b21–219a2 and 14 223a21–29. In this Plotinus seems to suggest that measures like minute or hour are not time itself but parts of time, derivatives of time and therein are not time itself. See III.7.9, 77–79: "And since time is and is said to be unlimited, how could there be number attached to it, unless one took a portion of it and measured the part; but time happened to exist in the part even before it came to be measured." Cf. III.7.12, 35–38: "For how could [time] measure time, if it is time, and what would it say as it was measuring, that it is as large as I am myself." On day and night as the means by which the Demiurge granted souls the ability to understand difference and, from there, number, see III.7.12, 30–34.

7, 7 *Nevertheless, if measuring. . . . whereas, if we were measuring according to the present, we would make it indivisible*: See III.7.12, 9–15 for the unified life of the one who has ascended to the eternal: ". . . if then we could imagine it as no longer active but this activity as put on hold and this part of the soul, too, turned back toward the intelligible world and eternity, and remaining still, what would there be after eternity? How could things differ from each other if everything rested in unity? How could there be a 'before'? How an 'after' or a 'future'? Where else could the soul cast its gaze other than where it is? Or rather not even here; for it would first have to stand apart from it in order to cast its gaze on it."

7, 8–10 *Now it is not unusual . . . what is present*: Cf. III.7.4, 25–28: "For the substantial existence of things that have come into being seems to be their point of origin, their coming to be, until the end of their time, in which they cease to exist; this is their 'is' and if anyone takes this away, their life-span is lessened, and so is their being."

7, 12 *For well-being requires continuance . . . than the present*: The use of *summenēkenai* is unclear insofar as translated as "continuation" or even "persistence" (see Armstrong) is a bit misleading. Both translations connote a sense of temporality. However, the etymological connection to that which holds together or remains together seems to be more apt. Gerson follows the MSS, substitutes *symbebēkenai*, and translates as follows: "For being happy requires that it occur . . . ," which may speak more to the necessity of well-being. Nevertheless, Gerson's translation loses something of the life of eternity. Kalligas (2014, 190) also seems to suggest that such a translation could work, but he too refrains from endorsing it positively. See further Alekniené (2010). Translation issues aside, overall, the point Plotinus is trying to make revolves around the idea that well-being and the present are measured by an absolute marker that remains in a complete state, while time and its movement require that it always retain a connection to what has come and gone.

7, 14–21 *Indeed, on the . . . altogether in it*: See *Timaeus* 37c6–38b5, where Plato lays the groundwork for this far-reaching analysis of the distinction between time and eternity. Here the eternal (*aidion*) is described as unchanging and grasped solely by intellect (27d–28a, 29a), and, most importantly for the later Neoplatonic relationship between Being, Life, and Intellect, is described as an Intelligible Living Thing (30c). Further, in the *Timaeus*, "was" and "will be" apply properly only to the sensible world, while "is" is all that can be said of the intelligible living model (37e–38a). Notoriously, time is defined by Plato as the "moving image of eternity" (30d). As an *image*, time replicates eternity in its everlasting movement and is "an eternal image, moving according to number . . ." (30d). Overall, Plotinus adopts this view, setting his theory of time apart from the Stoics and the Peripatetics by emphasizing eternity and time as, respectively, more than the whole of time or sensible movement. Both are instead a kind of processive and dynamic power, the life of Being and Soul. For more on the different forms of life of eternity and time, see III.7.6, 43–50: "But something that does not need what comes next, which is not measured in relation to another time or time which is unlimited and will exist unlimitedly, but is in possession of what it must be, this is what our conception is striving for; and its existence is not derived from a particular extent of time, but is prior to a particular extent. For it is appropriate to it that it is not of a certain quantity and has no contact at all with quantity to prevent its life being divided into parts and it losing its pure indivisibility and to ensure its remaining indivisible in its life and substantiality." III.7.3, 13–23: "If, then, you actually assemble them again into one so that there is one life together in them, concentrating Difference together with inexhaustible activity, Identity that is never different, and no intellection or life that goes from one thing to another, but a state of stability and constant lack of extension; when you have seen all this, you have seen eternity. It is when you have seen life abiding forever in the identical state and possessing everything in its presence, not now this, again something else, but all at once, and not now some things, now others, but a partless perfection; it is just as in a point where all things are together and none of them ever flows forth but remains in identity in itself and never changes, being always in the present because nothing of it has slipped away or again will come to be, but what it is is what it is." See Parmenides, fr. 8 lines 5–6, 36–37 for the premier Pre-Socratic precursor to this idea of eternity. For Aristotle on eternity, see *De Caelo* 279a23–25.

7, 21–22 *So if well-being is . . . is the best*: Cf. I.4.3, 27–28; III.2.3, 31, VI.6.18, 13. Here I have opted for something closer to Gerson's translation as opposed to Armstrong's "being," as the former reinforces the Plotinian idea of true existence as the best existence. Consider III.7.6, 29–34 where Plotinus clearly lays out the nature of existence as always already assuming eternity: "For there is no difference between 'that which is' and 'that which always is' just as there is no difference between 'philosopher' and 'true philosopher.' But because of the existence of the pretense to philosophy, there came about the addition of 'true' to 'philosopher.' For this reason, 'always' is added to 'that which is' and when you add 'always' to what 'is' you get 'that which always is' [*aei on*]." Nevertheless, we could have here a testimony to the relationship between being and life that the later Neoplatonists will be keen to explicate more fully.

7, 22–30 *So then it [. . .] all at once*: For a strong account of how the complete life is the eternal life that is fully present and not venturing outside itself, be it in the unfolding of life toward the future or the past, see III.7.5, 25–28: "And if someone were in this way to speak of eternity as a life which is here and now endless because it is total and expends nothing of itself, since it has no past or future—for if it had, it would not now be a total life—he would be near defining it." Interestingly, Plotinus is appealing to and transforming the Aristotelian notion of a complete life by utilizing this definition of eternity. Kalligas (2014, 191) notes the comparative uses of *adiastaton* at III.7.2, 32–35, 3.15–17, 36–38 as well as Sorabji (1989, 113).

Chapters 8 and 9

Returning to the role that memory plays in human well-being, Plotinus is quick to point out the contradictions of augmenting present well-being with past well-being. He does this by appealing the Epicurean idea that past pleasure/virtue can be utilized in the present moment to sustain one's present well-being. Recalling that for Epicurus "the greatest good is phronesis" (Diogenes Laertius, Lives of the Eminent Philosophers *10.1552) insofar as* phronesis *is that which is utilized to decipher the highest pleasure unmixed with pain, Plotinus appeals to a wholly other form of* phronesis *that is irreducible to a hedonistic calculus. This Epicurean* phronesis, *despite its desire for complete pleasure, would itself be incomplete, as it would only be concerned with particular choices and actions. The following, then, serves to juxtapose complete and perfect virtue or* phronesis *with incomplete Epicurean* phronesis*/pleasure. Moreover, Chapter 9 amends the Epicurean use of memory by returning to the distinction between the intelligible recollection of things like the Beautiful itself in contrast to the memory of past beautiful actions, which serve no part in the life of the one who has achieved well-being.*

8, 1–6 *But if someone says . . . to the hypothesis*: For the identification of "someone" as "Epicurus" see Diogenes Laertius, *Lives of the Eminent Philosophers* 10.11552. Plotinus, in this passage, explicitly appeals to the ambiguity of memory and the limits of human well-being. The question of how a memory can give more to what one already has at its fullest is dismissed as nonsensical. Basically, he is refuting the idea of increase via a simple calculation whereby in the present moment a person exhibits *phronesis* in its completion, suggesting that adding a memory of past virtue in its full completion would enhance one's well-being. There are two contradictions here to which Plotinus appeals. First, one cannot add to what is already complete, that is, true *phronesis* has a limit. In other words, if one is truly virtuous, adding the memory of it should not make it more. If it is making one more virtuous, then the memory augments what was, apparently, incomplete and therein the hypothesis is self-contradictory—one was apparently *not* in possession of full and perfect *phronesis* prior to remembering the instance of past *phronesis*, resulting in the fact that in the past one was more virtuous than in the present. Indeed, if one possessed complete *phronesis* in the present one need not have the memory of it in the past, because the past and present would be equal. The second contradiction results from the fact that since Plotinus locates human well-being in the intelligible world, talk of memory of the past, even past virtue, will be eradicated. See IV.4.1, 1–17. See Dillon (1996, 326). On a kind of memory which results from the natural disposition of the soul, see IV.4.4, 9. On such intellectual knowledge that results from recollection, see IV.4.5.

8, 6–11 *If it is the memory of pleasure . . . one was wise*: See Plutarch, *That Epicurus Actually Makes the Pleasant Life Impossible* 18 1099D (= fr. 436 Us), where he observes that for the Epicurean memory of past enjoyments contributes to present pleasure. Cf. Cicero, *Tusculan Disputations*, 5.96. See Linguiti (2016, 191n12), who argues that Plotinus' rejection of past pleasure being able to increase current pleasure puts the Neoplatonist paradoxically in agreement with the hedonist Aristippus, who also rejected the role memory plays in human well-being. See Diogenes Laertius, *Lives of the Eminent Philosophers* 2.89 (= fr. 453 Us). Furthermore, Plotinus is building from the preceding rebuttal and is less concerned with refuting the value of pleasure and the desire for excess, an always wanting more, than with the nature of corporeal imaginative memory and what it can bring to human well-being, whether it be a memory of pleasure or past virtue, or, as is the case with the Epicureans, the identity of virtue and pleasure. Recalling that pleasure concerns the body-soul composite, Plotinus would appeal to the forgetfulness of everything that derives from bodily sensation (cf. IV.3.26, 45–57). Memory of past sensible pleasure would ultimately be diminished via time and would be but a trace of itself, hence why it is ridiculous to believe that past pleasure experienced in eating a fine dish, whether yesterday or ten years ago, would contribute to happiness. Cf. IV.3.28, 17, where past enjoyment or fear is described as "a trace of the event deposited in [the faculty of appetite]."

This diminishment or forgetfulness of past pleasure/virtue is pervasive. It is demanded both at the level of the good life lived here, that is, the life that may remember past pleasure/virtue, but forgetfulness is also part of well-being. The former is a forgetfulness of the past experienced in time while the latter is achieved in the intelligible, allowing for a kind of forgetting of temporal activity altogether (see above notes on Chapter 1).

Kalligas (2014, 191) notes the use of *pericharia*, which appeals to the Platonic conception of pleasure as excess in the *Philebus* 65d8. See I.4.12, 5, where Plotinus also emphasizes that the good person would not suffer from such extreme pleasure. See Commentary on 9, 1–4 on the ambiguity of such pronouncements in relation to a kind of pleasure experienced by one who has ascended to a vision of the Beautiful.

9, 1–4 . . . *memory of the past*: His rhetorical question about the value of beautiful things orients his readers to memory of the forms—the truly beautiful things. Again, this is an appeal not to the memory of the body-soul composite by which it remembers sensual experience, as this form of memory leads to the forgetfulness of what one truly is. Rather, memory or recollection of the beautiful is the contrast being made here. See III.5.1, 59–63, where Plotinus discusses the difference between those who admire sensible beauty as opposed to those who recall it and are therein able to admire true Beauty as well as sensible beauty insofar as it is the "fulfillment of beauty there and its playful expression." Cf. I.3.1, 20–2, 15 on the ascent to true beauty from particular to absolute. This vision of the Beautiful is often described as the goal of all intellectual activity, a goal that is notably accompanied, according to the arguments of I.6.7, 13–14, with a kind of excessive pleasure that is not to be confused with sensual pleasure: "If anyone sees it, what passion will he feel, what longing in his desire to be united with it, what shock of delight!" and a bit later at 24–28: "If then one sees That which provides for all and remains by itself and gives to all but receives nothing into itself, if he abides in the contemplation of this kind of beauty and rejoices in being made like it, how can he need any other beauty?" While appealing to the value of this vision or recollection, Plotinus is quick to add that if one needs to turn to a particular memory of the rational or sensible sort, then one is presently lacking a vision of the Beautiful itself and, as such, could not be in a state of well-being. In other words, one is not currently recollecting the beautiful but is still in need of such recollection or instruction; one is only remembering a particular beauty.

On *anamnesis* as atemporal and therein consistent with his theory of well-being, see IV.3.25, 12–34, where he defends his position against the idea that the intelligible is in any way associated with memory of the sensible, particular sort. See Blumenthal (1971, 95–99).

Returning to I.5.9, Kalligas (2014, 191) refers to the *Philebus* 65e1–7 so as to clarify the identity of beauty and *phronesis*. Consider also Plotinus' emphasis in IV.7.10, 51–53 that once the soul has turned within, purifying itself from that which is not itself, it would "reflect that it had no need, after all, of beauty imported from without, since it itself emerged as supreme, provided that one let it be by itself."

Chapter 10

The final chapter in this short treatise is directly aimed at Aristotle (cf. Nicomachean Ethics *1098a32–1099a3) where he emphasizes that happiness is a disposition that must be made manifest: "For a man may possess the disposition without it producing any good result, as for instance when he is asleep, or has ceased to function from some other cause; but virtue in active exercise cannot be inoperative—it will of necessity act, and act well . . ." (trans. Rackham). Plotinus will fully refute the necessity of action (as normally understood) for the good life. Furthermore, in this section Plotinus takes one last shot at refuting the Aristotelian conception of pleasure as following from the fulfillment of virtue, as the necessary accompaniment of fulfilling one's proper work. Rather, for Plotinus any pleasure we derive is from the disposition (and therein not an affection coming from the external or caused by what is external but is something internal and inherent to the unification of the self with intellect), which is already perfect, rather than the action. Cf.* Nicomachean Ethics *1177b26–1178a8. Moreover, as Remes (2006) also argues, this discussion of the priority of contemplation over action constitutes a further charge against the Stoics, who would have regarded just actions as necessary for the sage.*

10, 1–10 *But [one might argue] length of time . . . with more actions*: Again, this is directed at 1098a18–20, where Aristotle writes that the good life is conditioned by the complete or full life: "Moreover this activity must occupy a complete lifetime; for one swallow does not make spring, nor does one fine day; and similarly one day or a brief period of happiness does not make a man supremely blessed and happy." Plotinus appeals to the past and its addition to the present as an addition of what is not to what is, reinforcing the idea that the singularity of the present is all that is required for human well-being. Furthermore, by appealing to fine actions, Plotinus is already setting up his rebuttal against the priority of action over contemplation. See below.

10, 10–14 *First of all then, . . . happy without actions*: See Remes (2006, 6) for a detailed account of the implications of this passage. On the limited nature of action in contradistinction to the person of contemplation, see III.8.4, 31–39: "Human beings, too, when they are weak in contemplation, produce action as a shadow of contemplation and reason. For their faculty of contemplation is not adequate for them due to weakness of soul, and being unable to grasp adequately the object of their vision and because of this not being filled [by it], yet still desirous of seeing it, they are carried towards action so that they can see [with their eyes] what they cannot see with their intellect." In other words, virtuous actions are but a pale image of the life of well-being.

See also VI.8.5, 1–36, where Plotinus clearly outlines the ambiguity of virtuous action that derives from external circumstances, for example courage in the face of war or justice as a consequence of having to repair an injustice. Another similar passage can be found at the early treatise V.9.1, 10–16 (quoted in the Introduction, pp. 25–26). Here, one may refer to Dillon (1996, 324), who argues that the Plotinian sage may fail to notice the old lady who needs help crossing the road and may further even fail to notice if "she were squashed by a passing wagon." Contra this, see Remes (2006), who persuasively argues that the Plotinian sage will act but that his virtue is not dependent upon his actions; his actions rather follow from his disposition. She emphasizes passages like I.4.15, which show that the sage will be friendly and predisposed to assist others in ascending to the life of the Intellect. As Remes (2006, 16) argues: "There is something in the wise man which makes him good to the people around him even though his directedness is simultaneously towards inner wisdom, and even though he is not motivated by emotions. Insofar as he treats his friends as he treats himself, his ethical deliberation is not purely agent-centered. In fact, the wise man would have a calling to live and work among other people, for Plotinus maintains that after union with the One, the soul must 'come and announce, if it could, to another that transcendent union' (VI.9.7, 20–28). A philosopher who has gone through Plotinian self-reformation will go back to the cave to teach others what he has seen.

The wise man has a duty to help others to achieve the same wisdom and virtue he himself has attained." See also Smith (1996, 229). Cf. VI.9.7, 28–35, where Plotinus insinuates that only the sage can truly help another because the sage, in contrast to others who flee from reality into the corporeal, are outside themselves and have destroyed themselves so that "they cannot look for someone else, any more than a child which is beside itself with madness knows its father." In other words, while the sage may seem disinterested and otherworldly, the sage, unlike others of incomplete virtue, actually sees the real self in others and can therein assist others in a way not feasible for those attached to the corporeal. See also II.9.9, 74–76 for Plotinus' emphasis on not looking to our individual interests. Cf. Porphyry, *Life of Plotinus* 8, where Porphyry seems to describe Plotinus in these terms. To return to passage III.8.4, 31–39, where actions are but pale images of the good of the intellect, the sage, unlike persons of this world, will be able to reproduce virtuous action in conformity with the unity and identity of the intelligible. See IV.4.44, 25–32 for another passage indicating that the actions of the good person derive from knowledge. Cf. III.8.6, 1–3 and 10, where Plotinus reinforces the idea that action is for the sake of contemplation or turns back to contemplation so that the person of perfect contemplation acts, but this person's acts are always but a return to the form of the good expressed in action.

10, 15–18 *The saving of . . . about through another*: Here, the pleasure of the wise needs to be situated within the pleasure that is not to be confused with bodily pleasure, but something more like the pleasure one experiences in contemplation of the beautiful at I.6.7, 13–28 or VI.7.30, 15–16. Action is not what produces this pleasure but unity with the object of thought. Thereby, in this passage, Plotinus is reinforcing the contemplative priority of the truly virtuous person insofar as it does not depend on the actions being one's own but rather on the form of the action, *ergo* why the contemplator need not be the source of the good action. Otherwise, such an individual is more concerned for their own good than concerned with understanding the good itself. In other words, Plotinus is directly showing how even the actions of those who are foolish are transformed by the Plotinian sage. The sage can see the reality and origin of the action in the One/Good and, as such, combines the various and disparate actions of individuals into a unity, seeing the world as that which returns to the form or being of things as they actually are. Overall, this widens the scope of the Plotinian sage as one not merely concerned for their own well-being but one who can see the possibility of well-being in others if only they would choose to see the true source of their actions. See II.9.9, 28 for the importance of the Plotinian sage being able to recognize that others are capable of virtue. Cf. VI.8.6, 10–18, where Plotinus insinuates that the truly virtuous person, that is, the person who has separated from the goings-on of the body-soul composite, may even retain their virtue despite doing things that ostensibly seem vicious, including abandoning one's children or country. In this, Plotinus is emphasizing that it is not the actions of the virtuous person that are to be judged but the character, the inner disposition so that it need not matter if someone else "saves the country" or if one abandons one's country. The life of the truly wise person is not dependent on external circumstances. Cf., however, Cicero, *De finibus* 3.32, where it is always an error to abandon one's country.

10, 19–24 *Rather, it is . . . that well-being consists*: Again, see VI.8.5, where Plotinus dismisses the idea that practical action and acting virtuously are truly in our power, as they are dependent upon circumstances. Rather, Plotinus emphasizes that the good of such acts are in the will and reason prior to the circumstances that support virtuous activity. Nevertheless, in contrast to the Stoics and Aristotle, this reason is not of this world but is the active intellect residing within. In this, Plotinus further emphasizes that this virtue is a state or disposition that intellectualizes the soul (VI.8.5, 20–37):

> If, then, virtue, being active in actions, were forced to help, how would it have the "up to it" in a pure fashion? Would we call the actions necessary, but the willing, and the reasoning before the actions not necessary?

In fact, if so, then, in positing these attributes in the bare factor prior to the thing done, we will posit autonomy and being up to virtue itself outside the action.

> What is, then, up to virtue itself, as a habit and disposition? Should we not say it comes to order the badly disposed soul, by bringing measure to affective states and desires? How, then, will we say being good and "virtue without master" are up to us?
>
> In fact, insofar as it is willed and chosen. Or, because, when it has come about in us, it constitutes freedom and the "up to us" and does not permit us still to be the slaves of what we were slaves to before. If, then, virtue is in a way another intellect and a habit which makes the soul rational, then again being up to us does not belong to us in action, but to intellect detached from actions.

Interestingly, in this passage we see the difference between the virtue that is disposed toward care for the body, that is, the soul corrupted by the body, and the virtue which is the disposition toward intellect. In other words, like I.5, Plotinus in VI.8.5 is attempting to transform our common conception of virtue based upon his schema in I.2.

Select Bibliography

I. Ancient Authors

ARISTOTLE: *De Anima*, translated by W. S. Hett. Loeb Classical Library. Cambridge, MA: Harvard University Press, 1957.

Nicomachean Ethics, translated by H. Rackham. Loeb Classical Library. Cambridge, MA: Harvard University Press, 1926.

DIOGENES LAERTIUS: *Lives of the Eminent Philosophers*, translated by R. D. Hicks. 2 vols. Loeb Classical Library. Cambridge, MA: Harvard University Press, 1925.

EPICUREA, edited by H. Usener. Leipzig, 1887.

LUCRETIUS: *On the Nature of Things*, translated by W. H. D. Rouse and M. Smith. Loeb Classical Library. Cambridge, MA: Harvard University Press, 1924.

MARCUS AURELIUS: *Meditations*, translated by C. R. Haines. Loeb Classical Library. Cambridge, MA: Harvard University Press, 1916.

PLUTARCH: *Moralia*, Volume XIII, translated by H. Cherniss. Loeb Classical Library. Cambridge, MA: Harvard University Press, 1976.

SENECA: *Epistles* 65–99, translated by R. Gummere. Loeb Classical Library. Cambridge, MA: Harvard University Press, 1917.

STOICORUM VETERUM FRAGMENTA, edited by H. von Arnim. Berlin/Boston: De Gruyter, 1903–1905.

II. Editions and Translations of the Enneads

Armstrong, A. H. 1966–1982. *Plotinus, Enneads*. Greek Text with English Translation and Introductions. 7 vols. Cambridge, MA: Loeb.

Bréhier, Émile. 1924–1938. *Plotin, Ennéades*. Greek Text and French Translation with Introductions and Notes. 7 vols. Paris: Les Belles Lettres.

Brisson, Luc and Jean François Pradeau, eds. 2002–2010. *Plotin Traités*. French Translation and Introductions. 8 vols. Paris: Flammarion.

Cilento, Vincenzo. 1947–1949. *Plotino, Enneadi*. Italian Translation and Commentary. 3 vols. Bari: Laterza.

Creuzer, Georg Friedrich. 1835. *Plotini Enneades*. Greek Text, with Marsilio Ficino's Latin Translation and Commentary. Oxford: E Typographeo Academico.

Gerson L. P., ed. 2018. *Plotinus, The Enneads.* Trans. Cambridge: Cambridge University Press.

Harder, Richard, Beutler, Robert, and Theiler, Willy. 1956–1971. *Plotins Schriften.* Greek Text with German Translation and Commentary. 12 vols. Hamburg: Meiner.

Henry, Paul and Schwyzer, Hans-Rudolph. 1951–1973. *Plotini Opera* I–III (editio maior). Paris: Desclée de Brouwer et Cie (HS_1).

———. 1964–1982. *Plotini Opera* I–III (editio minor, with revised text). Oxford: Clarendon Press (HS_2).

———. 1973. *Addenda et Corrigenda ad textum et apparatum lectionum.* In HS_1, t. III (HS_3).

———. 1982. *Addenda et Corrigenda ad textum et apparatum lectionum.* In HS_2, t. III (HS_4).

Igal, Jesus. 1982–1998. *Plotino, Enéadas.* 3 vols. Introduction, translations and notes. Madrid: Gredos.

Kalligas, P. 1994–2018. *Plotinus Enneads.* Text and Commentary in modern Greek. 6 vols. Athens: Akademia Athinon.

———. 2014. *The Enneads of Plotinus: A Commentary.* Vol. 1. Trans. E. Fowden and N. Pilavachi. Princeton/Oxford: Princeton University Press.

Kirchhoff, Adolph. 1856. *Plotini Opera.* Leipzig: Teubner.

Linguiti, A. 2000. *La felicità e il tempo. Plotino, "Enneadi" I 4–I 5. Introduzione, traduzione e commento.* Milano: LED Edizioni Universitarie.

MacKenna, Stephen. 19623. *Plotinus: The Enneads.* English Translation. Revised by B. S. Page. London: Faber & Faber.

———. 1991. *Plotinus. The Enneads.* Selected Treatises Revised with Notes by John Dillon. London: Penguin.

Schwyzer, Hans-Rudolph. 1987. "Corrigenda ad Plotini Textum." *Museum Helveticum* 44, 181–210 (HS_5).

III. Studies on Ennead I.5 and related works

Alekniené, T. 2010. "Plotin, Traité 36 (I 5), 7, 12: peut-on conserver la leçon des manuscrits συμβεβηκέναι?" *Hermes* 138/4, 494–501.

Baltzly, D. 2004. "The virtues and 'becoming like god': Alcinous to Proclus." *Oxford Studies in Ancient Philosophy* XXVI: 297–321. Oxford: Oxford University Press.

Baracat, José Carlos, 2013. "Soul's Desire and the Origin of Time in the Philosophy of Plotinus." In *Literary, Philosophical, and Religious Studies in the Platonic Tradition,* edited by J. Phillips and J. Finamore, 25–42. Sankt Augustin: Akademic Verlag.

Blumenthal, H. J. 1971. *Plotinus' Psychology. His Doctrines of the Embodied Soul*. The Hague: Martinus Nijhoff.

Ciapalo, R. T. 1987. *Life in Plotinus' Explanation of Reality*. PhD thesis. Chicago: Loyola University Chicago.

———. 1997. "The Relation of Plotinian Eudaimonia to the Life of the Serious Man in Treatise I. 4 (46)." *American Catholic Philosophical Quarterly* 71/3: 489–498.

Dillon, J. 1983. "Plotinus, Philo and Origen on the Grades of Virtue." In *Platonismus und Christentum. Festschrift für Heinrich Dörrie,* edited by H.-D. Blume and F. Mann, 92–105. Münster Westfalen.

———. 1996. "An Ethic for the Late Antique Sage." In *The Cambridge Companion to Plotinus*. Cambridge: Cambridge University Press.

Eliasson, E. K. 2008. *The Notion of That Which Depends on Us in Plotinus and Its Background*. Leiden: Brill.

Finamore, J. 2012. "Iamblichus on the Grades of Virtue." In *Iamblichus and the Foundations of Late Platonism*, edited by Afonasin, J. Dillon and J. Finamore, 113–132. Leiden: Brill.

Gerson, L. 2012. "Plotinus on Happiness." *Journal of Ancient Philosophy* 6, no. 1: 1–20.

Graeser, A. 1972. *Plotinus and the Stoics: A Preliminary Study*. Leiden: Brill.

Hadot, P. 1995. "'Only the Present is our Happiness': The Value of the Present Instant in Goethe and Ancient Philosophy." In *Philosophy as a Way of Life*, 217–237. Malden, MA: Blackwell Publishing.

Kalligas, P. 2000. "Living Body, Soul, and Virtue in the Philosophy of Plotinus." *Dionysius* 18: 25–38.

King, R. A. H. 2009. *Aristotle and Plotinus on Memory*. Berlin: De Gruyter.

Layne, D. A. 2019. "The Value of the Present Moment in Neoplatonic Philosophy." *Epoché: A Journal for the History of Philosophy* 25, no 2: 445–460.

Linguiti, A. 2016. "Plotinus and Epicurus on pleasure and happiness." In *Plotinus and Epicurus: Matter, Perception and Pleasure,* edited by A. Longo and D. Taormina, 189–198. Cambridge: Cambridge University Press.

Long, A. A. and Sedley, D. N. 1987. *The Hellenistic Philosophers: Vol. 1 Translations of the Principal Sources with Philosophical Commentary*. Cambridge: Cambridge University Press.

Majumdar, D. 2007. *Plotinus on the Appearance of Time and the World of Sense*. Aldershot: Ashgate Publishing.

Marsola, M. P. 2016. "'Heavy Birds' in tr. 5 (*Enn.* V 9) 1.8: References to Epicureanism and the problem of pleasure in Plotinus." In *Plotinus and Epicurus: Matter, Perception and Pleasure,* edited by A. Longo and D. Taormina, 82–95. Cambridge: Cambridge University Press.

McGroarty, K. 2006. *Plotinus on Eudaimonia: A Commentary on Ennead I. 4.* Oxford: Oxford University Press.

Plass, P. 1982. "Plotinus' Ethical Theory." *Illinois Classical Studies* 7: 241–259.

Perl, E. 2006. "The Togetherness of Thought and Being: A Phenomenological Reading of Plotinus' Doctrine 'That the Intelligibles Are Not outside the Intellect.'" *Proceedings of the Boston Area Colloquium in Ancient Philosophy* 22: 1–26.

Remes, P. 2006. "Plotinus' ethics of disinterested interest." *Journal of the History of Philosophy* 44: 1–23.

———. 2008. *Plotinus on Self: The Philosophy of the 'We.'* Cambridge: Cambridge University Press.

Smith, A. 1996. "Eternity and Time." In *The Cambridge Companion to Plotinus,* edited by L. Gerson, 196–216. New York: Cambridge University Press.

———. 1999. "The Significance of Practical Ethics in Plotinus." In *Traditions of Platonism,* edited by J. Cleary, 335–344. Aldershot: Ashgate Publishing.

———. 2005. "Action and Contemplation in Plotinus." In *Philosopher and Society in Late Antiquity. Essays in Honour of Peter Brown,* edited by A. Smith, 65–72. Swansea: Classical Press of Wales.

Stamatellos, G. 2016. "Virtue and Hexis in Plotinus." *The International Journal for the Platonic Tradition* 9: 129–145.

Stern-Gillet, S. 2009. "Dual Selfhood and Self-Perfection in the Enneads." *Epoché: A Journal for the History of Philosophy* 13: 331–345.

Van Riel, G., 2000. *Pleasure and the Good Life: Plato, Aristotle and the Neoplatonists.* Leiden: Brill.

Viglas, K. 2006. "L'expérience de l'instant métaphysique: la contribution de Plotin au problème 'éternité et temps.'" *Philotheos* 6: 131–143.

Warren, E. 1965. "Memory in Plotinus." *The Classical Quarterly* 15, no. 2: 252–260.

IV. General Publications

Armstrong, A. H. 1940. *The Architecture of the Intelligible Universe in the Philosophy of Plotinus.* Cambridge: Cambridge University Press.

Arnou, R. 1968. *Le Désir de Dieu dans la philosophie de Plotin.* 2nd ed. Rome: Presses de l'Université Grégorienne.

Dillon, J. 1977/1996. *The Middle Platonists: A Study of Platonism, 80 B.C.–A.D. 220,* London: Duckworth, 1977, 1996.

Dodds, Eric R. 1965. *Pagan and Christian in an Age of Anxiety: Some Aspects of Religious Experience from Marcus Aurelius to Constantine*. Cambridge: Cambridge University Press.

Emilsson, E. K. 1988. *Plotinus on Sense-Perception.* Cambridge: Cambridge University Press.

———. 2007. *Plotinus on Intellect.* Oxford: The Clarendon Press.

———. 2017. *Plotinus*. London: Routledge.

Gerson, L. P. 1994. *Plotinus.* London/New York: Routledge.

———, ed. 1996. *The Cambridge Companion to Plotinus.* Cambridge: Cambridge University Press.

———, ed. 2010. *The Cambridge History of Philosophy in Late Antiquity.* 2 vols. Cambridge: Cambridge University Press.

Hadot, Pierre. 1993. *Plotinus on the Simplicity of Vision.* Translated by M. Chase. Chicago: Chicago University Press.

Inge, W. R. 1948. *The Philosophy of Plotinus.* 3rd ed. London: Longmans, Green.

Lloyd, Anthony C. 1990. *The Anatomy of Neoplatonism.* Oxford: Clarendon Press.

O'Daly, G. 1973. *Plotinus' Philosophy of the Self.* Shannon: Irish University Press.

O'Meara, Dominic J. 1993. *Plotinus: an Introduction to the Enneads.* Oxford: Oxford University Press.

Remes, Pauliina. 2008. *Neoplatonism.* Berkeley: University of California Press.

Remes, Pauliina and Slaveva-Griffin, Svetla, eds. 2014. *The Routledge Handbook of Neoplatonism.* London: Routledge.

Rist, John M. 1967. *Plotinus: The Road to Reality.* Cambridge: Cambridge University Press.

Schniewind, Alexandrine. 2003. *L'Éthique du Sage chez Plotin.* Paris: J. Vrin.

Smith, Andrew. 2004. *Philosophy in Late Antiquity.* London: Routledge.

Wallis, R. T. 1995. *Neoplatonism.* 2nd ed. London: Duckworth.

Index of Ancient Authors

Index of Names and Subjects

• ALSO AVAILABLE FROM PARMENIDES PUBLISHING •

PRE-SOCRATICS

By Being, It Is: *The Thesis of Parmenides* by Néstor-Luis Cordero

The Fragments of *Parmenides*: *A Critical Text with Introduction and Translation, the Ancient Testimonia and a Commentary by A. H. Coxon. Revised and Expanded Edition edited with new Translations by Richard McKirahan and a new Preface* by Malcolm Schofield

The Legacy of Parmenides: *Eleatic Monism and Later Presocratic Thought* by Patricia Curd

Parmenides and the History of Dialectic: *Three Essays* by Scott Austin

Parmenides, Venerable and Awesome: *Proceedings of the International Symposium* edited by Néstor-Luis Cordero

Presocratics and Plato: *A Festschrift in Honor of Charles Kahn* edited by Richard Patterson, Vassilis Karasmanis, and Arnold Hermann

The Route of Parmenides: *Revised and Expanded Edition, With a New Introduction, Three Supplemental Essays, and an Essay* by Gregory Vlastos by Alexander P. D. Mourelatos

To Think Like God: *Pythagoras and Parmenides. The Origins of Philosophy. Scholarly and fully annotated edition* by Arnold Hermann

The Illustrated To Think Like God: *Pythagoras and Parmenides. The Origins of Philosophy* by Arnold Hermann (with over 200 full color illustrations)

PLATO

The Second Alcibiades: *A Platonist Dialogue on Prayer and on Ignorance* by Harold Tarrant

A Stranger's Knowledge: *Statesmanship, Philosophy, and Law in Plato's Statesman* by Xavier Márquez

God and Forms in Plato by Richard D. Mohr

Image and Paradigm in Plato's Sophist by David Ambuel

Imperial Plato: Albinus, Maximus, Apuleius by Ryan Fowler

Interpreting Plato's Dialogues by J. Angelo Corlett

One Book, the Whole Universe: *Plato's Timaeus Today* edited by Richard D. Mohr and Barbara M. Sattler

Platonic Patterns: *A Collection of Studies* by Holger Thesleff

Plato's Late Ontology: *A Riddle Resolved* by Kenneth M. Sayre

Plato's Parmenides: *Text, Translation & Introductory Essay* by Arnold Hermann. Translation in collaboration with Sylvana Chrysakopoulou with a Foreword by Douglas Hedley

Plato's Universe by Gregory Vlastos

ARISTOTLE

Aristotle's Empiricism: Experience and Mechanics in the Fourth Century B.C. by Jean De Groot

One and Many in Aristotle's Metaphysics—*Volume I: Books Alpha-Delta* by Edward C. Halper

One and Many in Aristotle's Metaphysics—*Volume 2: The Central Books* by Edward C. Halper

Reading Aristotle: Physics VII.3 "What is Alteration?" *Proceedings of the International ESAP-HYELE Conference* edited by Stefano Maso, Carlo Natali, and Gerhard Seel

HELLENISTIC PHILOSOPHY

A Life Worthy of the Gods: *The Materialist Psychology of Epicurus* by David Konstan

THE *ENNEADS* OF PLOTINUS

Translations with Introductions & Philosophical Commentaries
Series edited by John M. Dillon and Andrew Smith

Ennead **I.1:** ***What Is the Living Thing? What Is Man?*** by Gerard O'Daly

Ennead **I.6:** ***On Beauty*** by Andrew Smith

Ennead **II.5:** ***On What Is Potentially and What Actually*** by Cinzia Arruzza

Ennead **II.9:** ***Against the Gnostics*** by Sebastian Ramon Philipp Gertz

Ennead **II.4:** ***On Matter*** by; Anthony A. Long

Ennead **III.4:** ***On Our Allotted Guardian Spirit*** by Wiebke-Marie Stock

Ennead **IV.3–IV.4.29:** ***Problems concerning the Soul*** by John M. Dillon and H. J. Blumenthal

Ennead **IV.4.30–45 & IV.5:** ***Problems concerning the Soul*** by Gary M. Gurtler

Ennead **IV.7:** ***On the Immortality of the Soul*** by Barrie Fleet

Ennead **IV.8:** ***On the Descent of the Soul into Bodies*** by Barrie Fleet

Ennead **V.1:** ***On the Three Primary Levels of Reality*** by Eric D. Perl

Ennead **V.5:** ***That the Intelligibles are not External to the Intellect, and on the Good*** by Lloyd P. Gerson

Ennead **VI.4 & VI.5:** ***On the Presence of Being, One and the Same, Everywhere as a Whole*** by Eyjólfur Emilsson and Steven Strange

Ennead **VI.8:** ***On the Voluntary and on the Free Will of the One*** by Kevin Corrigan and John D. Turner

Ennead **VI.9:** ***On the Good or the One*** by Stephen R. L. Clark

ETHICS

Sentience and Sensibility: *A Conversation about Moral Philosophy* by Matthew R. Silliman

PHILOSOPHICAL FICTION

Pythagorean Crimes by Tefcros Michaelides

The Aristotle Quest: A Dana McCarter Trilogy. Book 1: Black Market Truth by Sharon M. Kaye

AUDIOBOOKS

The Iliad (unabridged) by Stanley Lombardo

The Odyssey (unabridged) by Stanley Lombardo

The Essential Homer by Stanley Lombardo

The Essential Iliad by Stanley Lombardo

FORTHCOMING

Ennead **I.2:** ***On Virtues*** by Suzanne Stern-Gillet

Ennead **I.3:** ***On Dialectic*** by Pauliina Remes

Ennead **I.4:** ***On Well-Being*** by Kieran McGroarty

Ennead **I.8:** ***On the Nature and Source of Evil*** by Anne Sheppard

Ennead **I.9:** ***On Going Out of the Body*** by Suzanne Stern-Gilet

Ennead **II.1:** ***On the Heavens by*** Andrew Smith

Ennead **II.6:** ***On Substance, or On Quality*** by Damien Caluori

Ennead **II.7:** ***On Complete Blending*** by Robert Goulding

Ennead **II.8:** ***On Sight*** by Robert Goulding

Ennead **III.5:** ***On Love*** by Sara Magrin

Ennead **III.6:** ***On Impassibility*** by Eleni Perdikouri

Ennead **III.7:** ***On Eternity and Time*** by László Bene

Ennead **III.8:** ***On Nature and Contemplation*** by George Karamanolis

Ennead **IV.6:** ***On Sense-Perception and Memory*** by Peter Lautner

Ennead **IV.9:** ***On Whether All Souls are One*** by Eyjólfur Emilsson

Ennead **V.2, V.4, and V.6:** ***On the One and Intellect*** by Eleni Perdikouri

Ennead **V.3:** ***On the Knowing Hypostases*** by Marie-Élise Zovko

Ennead **V.9:** ***On Intellect, Ideas, and Being*** by Matthias Vorwerk

Ennead **VI.1-2:** ***On the Genera of Being (I+II)*** by Damien Caluori and Regina Füchslin

Ennead **VI.3:** ***On the Genera of Being (III)*** by Riccardo Chiaradonna

Ennead **VI.7:** ***The Forms and the Good*** by Nicholas Banner